SETTING GOALS
THAT COUNT

SETTING GOALS THAT COUNT

A Christian Perspective

Joseph D. Allison

Published by

chosen books
of The Zondervan Corporation
Grand Rapids, Michigan 49506

Unless otherwise noted, all Scripture quotations are taken from the New American Standard Bible, copyright 1977 by the Lockman Foundation, LaHabra, California.

Library of Congress Cataloging in Publication

Allison, Joseph D.

  Setting goals that count.

    1. Christian life—1960- 2. Goal (Psychology)

I. Title.

BV4501.2.A435 1984   248.4   84-14670

ISBN 0-310-60941-0

Chosen Books is a division of The Zondervan Corporation, Grand Rapids, Michigan 49506. Editorial offices for Chosen Books are in Lincoln, Virginia 22078.

85 86 87 88 89 90 / 9 8 7 6 5 4 3 2 1

To my daughter, Heather—
She has waited long enough
for Dad to finish his book
and come downstairs.

Contents

Preface

The people in the congregation I used to pastor in Fort Wayne, Indiana, often heard me say I was giving them sermons that I needed to hear. In this case, I have given you a book that I needed to read.

I have concluded that the ultimate measure of Christian obedience is not what we do; it's what we become. So while writing this book, I reexamined what sort of person I am becoming for the Lord.

My self-examination revealed a character much in need of maturing. It uncovered attitudes that shamed me. But it also fired my heart with a yearning to "attain . . . to a mature man, to the measure of the stature which belongs to the fullness of Christ" (Ephesians 4:13).

If the Lord uses this book to kindle such a yearning in your heart, it will have accomplished its purpose.

Joseph D. Allison
Grand Rapids, Michigan

We are always getting ready to live, but never living.

Ralph Waldo Emerson

1

Are You Setting Goals— Or Just Making Plans?

A troubled man poured out his frustrations to a Christian friend. He had made a career of government service—over twenty years so far—and he had "peaked" early. Promotions eluded him. Regulations hamstrung him. Yet he said, "If I can hang on just a few more years I'll be able to retire. I don't want to lose my benefits."

His friend listened patiently.

"I feel that I'm at a dead end," the man went on. "So many days I just want to park my truck and walk away from it all—from the job, the family, everything. I feel trapped, and I don't know how to get out."

"How old are you?"

"Fifty-three."

"Not that old. And you're in good health. Barring any accidents or unexpected illnesses, you should live past the average life expectancy for a man. That's about age 70. How old were your grandfathers when they died?"

"They were both in their mid-eighties."

"Then the statistics say you'll probably live to your eighties, too." His friend did a quick mental computation. "That means you may have nearly thirty years of healthy, productive life ahead of you. One-third of your life is still ahead of you. *So what are you doing the rest of your life?"*

"You know, I really haven't given it much thought," the man replied.

This man's predicament is all too common among Christians. In our rush to make a livelihood, we have forgotten our goals for life. So when we come to a critical juncture, such as the last decade before retirement, we feel anxiety and fear. We don't know where we're going. We have no long-range goals.

This is why I believe we should study what God's Word says about our life goals. How does God say we should set long-range goals? How does He say we can reevaluate our goals when life changes drastically and unexpectedly? These are the questions we will tackle in this book.

You will find some practical tools for goal-setting, as well as step-by-step procedures for reevaluating your life goals at crucial decision points, such as this government worker was facing. More important, you will be challenged to consider how your daily plans fit into the big picture of lifelong goals. You will gain a fresh perspective on the way God reveals His will to you. In short, this is more than a nuts-and-bolts manual of life planning; it's an invitation to reassess your relationship with God.

A Christian does his goal-setting and plan-making within the context of this relationship, while a non-Christian sets goals and makes crucial decisions without the benefit of this relationship. We will come back to this matter repeatedly, and you will test your aspirations against Scripture to see whether they are godly aspirations. Because I'm convinced that *a person feels most satisfied when he strives to become the person God created him to be.*

Thus, a personal relationship with God—intimate communion with Him—is essential to goal-setting. Throughout this book, I will call you to reexamine your relationship with Him.

Goals vs. Plans

First, we ought to understand the difference between a goal and a plan. We often get the two confused.

On New Year's Day, people customarily make resolutions for the year ahead. Most of those resolutions are not goals; they are plans. That is to say, they are *methods for reaching a goal.* I might tell you, for example, "I have a goal of losing weight this year."

"Exactly what do you have in mind?" you might ask.

"Well, I'm going to eat no more than a thousand calories a day." (That's not a goal; it's a plan. It's how I'm going to act in order to reach my goal.)

"How much weight do you hope to lose?" you ask.

"About thirty pounds." (Again, that's not a goal; it's a plan. It's a strategy for reaching my goal.)

So you press me. "Why do you want to lose thirty pounds?"

"So that I'll be healthier," I say. "So that my body will be stronger. Perhaps I'll even live a bit longer by taking off some excess weight."

Now *that* is a goal! It is the end toward which I am aiming. It is the destination I am trying to reach. All the other steps—the menus, the exercise routines, the targets for each week's weight loss—are simply the means for reaching my ultimate destination. That destination is my real goal.

For this reason, you aren't too upset if you forget your New Year's resolutions by Ground Hog's Day. You probably don't wring your hands and say, "Oh, dear, I've really failed!" Because resolutions are not really your goals; they are simply plans for reaching your goals. And if one plan fails, you simply try another.

Here is a good way to tell the difference between a plan and a goal: *Generally, you describe plans with "do" sentences and goals with "be" sentences.* Here are some sample New Year's resolutions; see if you can tell whether they are goals or plans:

"I'm going to iron shirts every Monday morning."
"I'm going to visit Aunt Effie every week."
"I'm going to take a course in accounting."

These are "do" sentences. Each one describes your method or strategy for reaching a goal. Now look at these resolutions:

"I'm going to iron shirts every Monday morning *so that I'll be a more efficient homemaker.*"
"I'm going to visit Aunt Effie every week *so that I'll be a more faithful nephew.*"
"I'm going to take a course in accounting *so that I'll be a better bookkeeper.*"

See the difference? The "do" sentences described your plan of action, and the "be" sentences described the result of that action. Your plans are how you intend to reach your destination; but your goals *are* your destination. It is important to keep sight of the goal—what you intend to "be."

Instead of thinking about what you will do in the next year, think about *who you will become.* That really is your goal.

I believe many Christians act irresponsibly and impulsively because they are so busy with short-range plans that they don't take stock of their goals. Or they are so absorbed with the daily strategies of living that they forget about their goals. They don't know if they have reached today's goals or if they are any closer to tomorrow's. They are consumed with interest in what they're going to *do;* but they don't consider who they want to *become.*

I urge you to set goals before you start making plans.

Heart vs. Mind

God influences a Christian's goal-setting and plan-making. But He seldom does it through dreams, visions or signs. God generally influences you through what you might call an internal guidance system.

When engineers designed the Apollo spacecraft that took our astronauts to the moon, they gave it an internal guidance system. The astronauts coud not steer themselves to their destination a quarter of a million miles from earth. If they erred by even a fraction of an inch, they would miss the target by hundreds of miles.

So microcomputers and telemetry devices were stowed in the belly of that spacecraft to steer it. A control base monitored the flight, and the astronauts took navigation readings by the stars from time to time to make sure the guidance system was keeping them on course. But they left the "driving" to that ingenious little box of electronic hardware, the internal guidance system.

God has given every one of His servants an internal guidance system, too. It's not electronic. It doesn't use computer chips or cables. But it receives His guidance just as reliably as the Apollo guidance system did. The Bible calls this internal guidance system the "heart."

Granted, our hearts may sometimes go wrong. We must take readings against God's Word and the counsel of other Christians to make sure our hearts keep us on God's true course. But remember, *God steers a Christian through his heart.* So we should not be afraid to listen to our hearts— our innermost aspirations—because they can point us toward serving the Lord.

While Scripture uses the term *heart* to refer to our goalsetting, it uses the term *mind* to refer to our daily plan-making. One New Testament passage points out the difference between a person's heart and mind:

> This is the covenant that I will make with the house of Israel after those days, saith the Lord; I will put my laws into their mind, and write them in their hearts: and I will be to them a God, and they shall be to me a people.
>
> (Hebrews 8:10, KJV)

The Bible notes two distinct functions of the heart and mind. It says God will *put* His law into His people's minds and *write* it upon their hearts. The word *put* suggests temporary storage, while *write* indicates more permanent storage.

We still observe this distinction. How often we say, "I've changed my mind," yet how seldom we say, "I've changed my heart." The mind seems to be an easily changed, quickly reprogrammed part of our internal guidance system, while the heart seldom changes.

To carry out the spacecraft analogy, we could call the heart the "wired circuit" of our personal guidance system.

The mind is more like a floppy disk, quickly changed and reprogrammed.

The distinction between heart and mind reappears throughout the Bible. Scripture suggests that a person's heart guides what his mind thinks. An evil heart directs an evil mind, which devises evil schemes. Notice how the Bible describes the human race just before the Flood:

> And God saw that the wickedness of man was great in the earth, and that every imagination of the thoughts of his heart was only evil continually.
> (Genesis 6:5, KJV)

Fallen man had turned against God; he did not want to serve God. Note that Scripture says, "The thoughts of his heart [were] only evil. . . ." His evil thinking bubbled up from his evil heart.

Notice how the psalmist described a wicked person:

> Deliver me, O Lord, from the evil man: preserve me from the violent man; which imagine mischiefs [devise *evil* things, according to the NASV] in their heart; continually are they gathered together for war.
> (Psalm 140:1-2, KJV)

The psalmist knew that every ungodly person has the same basic problem—"heart disease." An evil person's heart is not right, so his life purpose is not right. As the King James puts it, he intends to make mischief with other people's lives. That ungodly purpose steers him. His every decision and plan springs from his mischievous heart.

We cannot expect that we, as basically selfish people, will act differently until God changes the goal-setting center of our lives. He can do that. He can give every one of us a new character and a new vision of our future.

Saul is a case in point. He was the son of a donkey-farmer. One day his father sent him out to look for some stray donkeys. He searched and searched without success and finally decided to consult the prophet Samuel, hoping he would know where the donkeys were. When Saul arrived at Samuel's house, however, the prophet knew God wanted this young man to lead the Israelites in battle against their enemies, the Philistines. So he announced that Saul's donkey-herding days were over—he was a soldier now!

Saul did not believe him. "Am I not a Benjamite," he asked, "of the smallest of the tribes of Israel? and my family the least of all the families of the tribe of Benjamin? wherefore then speakest thou so to me?" (I Samuel 9:21, KJV).

But the prophet knew God's goals for Saul. He predicted that God would give him several signs to prove he should take this new assignment.

First, Samuel said he would meet two men who would tell him to get along home—friends of his father who would warn Saul to go back to his donkeys. (Interesting! We tend to think that when God gives us new goals, He shuts the door to old opportunities. That wasn't so for Saul.)

Second, Saul would meet other strangers who would give him bread without his asking. We often think that when God calls us to do something, He will make us scrounge and scrimp for the means to do it, as if a call to God's work is confirmed by poverty. But that wasn't so for Saul.

Third, Saul would meet a band of prophets singing, dancing and prophesying as they traveled down the road. This was the strangest sign of all, for Samuel said: " . . . The Spirit of the Lord will come upon thee, and thou shalt prophesy with them, *and shalt be turned into another man*" (I Samuel 10:6, KJV, italics mine).

We often think that when God gives us new goals in life, He changes only our goals. But that wasn't so for Saul. When the Spirit of God came upon him, he became "another man." The shy, quiet farm boy turned into a whirling, singing prophet. So Saul's third sign of a God-given change in goals was a change in his personality.

All three signs came when Saul left the prophet's house, proving that God was calling him to be the captain of Israel. And notice verse 9:

> . . . When he had turned his back to go from Samuel, *God* gave *him another heart:* and all those signs came to pass that day.
>
> (I Samuel 10:9, KJV, italics mine)

Saul acted differently because God changed the very core of his life. He changed Saul by changing his heart— the seat of his goals and aspirations.

Unfortunately, Saul's heart changed again after he became king. He took up the high priest's duties, kept the spoils of battle, consulted the witch of Endor, and disobeyed the Lord in other flagrant ways. His personality did another about-face. He became impulsive, volatile and vain. The wizened prophet Samuel had to denounce him and announce the selection of a new king.

Though God had changed his internal guidance system, Saul was still at the controls of his life. He could choose to heed the dictates of his changed heart, or override them to suit more selfish purposes. Sadly, he chose the latter and turned his heart away from God to self-service and self-aggrandizement. He ignored the readings of his spiritual "instruments" and tried to follow his own perverse desires. In the process, he wrecked his life.

There are many other Old Testament examples of how God uses the heart to guide goal-making. But let's notice what the New Testament says about the heart.

Jesus taught that the heart guides our entire life (Matthew 12:34; Mark 7:21-23; Luke 6:43-45). The heart dictates what we say; it organizes what we think; it initiates what we do; it brings forth every emotion we feel. The heart is the switchboard at the center of our thoughts, feelings and actions. If we change our heart, we change our entire life.

Jesus condemned the evil things that come from the heart of an evil man, but commended the good things that come from the heart of a good man:

A good man out of the good treasure of his heart bringeth forth that which is good; and an evil man out of the evil treasure of his heart bringeth forth that which is evil: for out of the abundance of the heart his mouth speaketh.

(Luke 6:45, KJV)

What accounts for the difference? How do some people have hearts that honor the Lord?

A person's own choice accounts for the difference. Each one of us decides whether to receive or to shun God's transforming power. We decide whether to keep our rebellious heart or receive a loyal, obedient heart for God. When Gentiles began giving themselves to Jesus Christ, Peter said:

. . . God, who knows the heart, acknowledged them, by giving them the Holy Spirit just as He did to us.

(Acts 15:8, NKJV)

We often speak of someone "giving his heart to the Lord" when he is converted; and that is exactly what happens. A Christian is one who gives the goal-setting core of his life to God, allowing God to change it.

The apostle Paul wrote:

. . . The love of God has been poured out in our hearts by the Holy Spirit who was given to us.

(Romans 5:5, NKJV)

. . . God be thanked that though you were slaves of sin, yet you obeyed from the heart that form of doctrine to which you were delivered. And having been set free from sin, you became slaves of righteousness.

(Romans 6:17-18, NKJV)

What a dramatic change God worked in your life when you became a Christian! He began changing you at the very core of your life—the heart—so He could govern everything else you do. The love of God took control of your heart, drawing you to follow His Word. Though once you were a slave of self, you now are a "slave of righteousness." Your heart belongs to God; and your thoughts, attitudes and actions will bear this out.

The Bible reveals that your internal guidance system has two interrelated functions: the "heart function" (setting goals, forming your character) and the "mind function" (making daily plans to reach your goals). Your goals determine your plans; your heart steers your mind. And no matter how long or how grievously you have disobeyed God, He can transform your life by giving you a new heart with new goals.

A Developing Dream: Joseph

The transformation may not come in an instant. Your vision of the future may evolve over a period of months, even years, as God molds your heart. You may have no clear idea of your ultimate destination; you may see only the first step of change. But as you take each step (a plan), you get a better idea of where you're going (goal).

Do you remember how this happened with Joseph? While a young boy, Joseph dreamed that he would become superior to all his brothers, superior even to his parents. He would become a man of such great power and influence that they would bow down to him. What bombastic dreams those seemed to be! But over the next several years, Joseph realized God's plan for his life as . . .

. . . He was sold into slavery and carried into Egypt.
. . . He was thrown into prison for allegedly molesting an official's wife.
. . . He lay in prison fifteen years, forgotten by a prisoner he helped to free.

Only when he was called to interpret a dream for Pharaoh did he become one of the most powerful men in Egypt.

That's often how God deals with us: He gives us a snapshot of what He wants us to become. Then, step by step, He develops the details of that picture. In Isaiah 42:16, God says:

"I will lead the blind by a way they do not know, in

paths they do not know I will guide them. I will make darkness into light before them and rugged places into plains. . . ."

God says He will make the darkness into light before us, but He may do it just when we think we're stepping off into an abyss! He says He will make the rugged places plain, but He may not do so until we are ready to take that next step.

It reminds me of the way Jimmy Durante walked off the stage at the end of his old television program. All was darkness in the background as Durante started singing his theme song. Then a spotlight showed the first place he was to step. He walked into that spotlight, when another spotlight appeared—the next step he was to take. And so it went, the successive spots of light leading Durante off the stage.

"I will make the darkness into light before them," God says. How far before us? Perhaps just one step—when we're ready to take it. That way we have to follow Him by faith.

You may have a mental image—a "snapshot"—of the kind of person you believe God expects you to be, even though it may be poorly focused and fuzzy. On the other hand, you may have no idea of God's expectations for your life. You may feel like saying, "How do I trip the shutter and get a picture?"

In the following chapters, you will learn how. A series of questionnaires will focus your imagination on a vision of what your life can become for God's glory. One chapter will invite you to take stock of your abilities, and another will help you assess your spiritual gifts so that you know what equipment you have for developing the "snapshot" of your future.

Before we roll up our sleeves and enter the darkroom, though, we ought to deal with some pointed questions:

1. How will you know whether your goals are truly God-given?

2. How can you overcome the fear of change or the numbness of indecision in order to pursue your goals?

3. How can you know when it's time to take another step toward your goals?

We are going to take up these questions in the next four chapters.

Don't measure your potential with your own yardstick. Your life is no longer your own. Christ lives in you.

(Cf. Galatians 2:20)

2

How to Test Your Goals

When prospectors went West in the 1850s to search for gold, each one carried a vial of acid to test the nuggets he found. When he picked up a piece of ore that looked like gold, he would drip a little acid on it. If acid dissolved the ore, it wasn't really gold; it was "fool's gold" and worthless. But if the acid did nothing to the ore, the prospector knew he had found the real thing.

You ought to give your goals the acid test, too. But your acid is the Word of God. Hebrews 4:12 says:

The Word of God is living and active and sharper than any two-edged sword . . . and able to judge the thoughts and intentions of the heart.

That is how we will use the Word of God in this chapter—to judge the intentions of your heart. The Word will reveal whether they are godly intentions.

Here is the first Bible standard you can use to test your goals: *A godly goal will bring glory to God.*

As Sherlock Holmes would say, "That's elementary." But this standard is often overlooked. The carnal man strives for his own glory and honor and fame, and may even tell the Lord so. "After all," he says, "people will be so impressed with what I've done that they'll want to be Christians, too!"

But that is a lie. God's first priority is not to glorify us, but Himself. Do you remember the last declaration of the Lord's Prayer? After calling on His heavenly Father for guidance, food, forgiveness and protection, Jesus said,

> "For *Thine* is the kingdom, and the power, and the glory, forever."
>
> (Matthew 6:13)

God's primary purpose is to bring glory to Himself, although modern Christians are loath to accept the idea. We envision God as a cosmic valet peering over a distant cloud, waiting for some opportunity to help us. Do we need a job? A supernatural provision for the bills? A cure to some dreaded illness? We'll just ask the Lord and He will give us what we want.

But this attitude overlooks God's reason for helping us. It disregards the fact that God prospers and protects His people so that the rest of the world will realize what a great God He is. He helps us in order to confirm His own nature as our gracious Sovereign, not to confirm *our* nature as favored subjects.

The psalmist prayed, "For Thy name's sake Thou wilt lead me and guide me" (Psalm 31:3). He often had to call on the Lord for help. Why? To save his own skin? To build a spiritual reputation for himself? To spare himself biting words of criticism? He may have wanted all these things, but they did not move him to pray. He asked everything so that people would glorify God's name.

Ponder your goals for the future. Does each one bring glory to the Lord?

Would your dream home, for example, bring honor to God? Or would it make motorists park by the curb, gaze enviously at the facade and say, "Wow! They must be pretty successful to own a place like that!"

Consider your ideal vocation or career. Would it enable people to see that God is guiding and blessing you? Or would it cause them to praise your own knowledge and skill?

Examine your goals for your church. How well would your dream church glorify God? Would it really help you worship and serve the Lord? Or would it help mainly in impressing your friends?

You might say, "Wait a minute! No goals are in themselves either God-honoring or self-serving. A $500,000 home might honor the Lord or it might honor me. It all depends."

And so it does. It depends on your attitude toward your goals, which brings us back to the heart.

Is your heart set on serving God, no matter what job He gives you or what home He provides or what congregation He places you in? If serving Him is your deepest desire, then credit Him for every aspect of your future by being as grateful for those things that do not quite fit the modern image of success as you are for those things that do.

Does He give you a two-bedroom apartment instead of a four-bedroom house? If your heart is right, you thank Him. Does He give you one rattly station wagon instead of two sleek new sedans? You thank Him. When you fully delight yourself in the Lord, you want to have whatever He grants you for doing His will.

The second acid test for your goals is this: *A godly goal will bear fruit for the Lord.* The hope that someday you can simply enjoy God's blessings and stop bearing fruit for Him is not a godly goal. Paul wrote to his Christian friends at Thessalonica:

> We hear that some among you are leading an undisciplined life, doing no work at all, but acting like busybodies. Now such persons we command and exhort in the Lord Jesus Christ to work in quiet fashion and eat their own bread.
>
> (II Thessalonians 3:11-12)

Apparently the church at Thessalonica had its quota of pikers. So did the churches at Ephesus (I Timothy 5:13), Crete (Titus 1:10-13) and elsewhere (I Peter 4:15-17)—despite our piously embellished image of the first-century church. These people liked being spectators; they enjoyed the blessings of Christian fellowship, not to mention the food! And why should they work if they could leech what they needed from other Christians? They were fruit-eaters but not fruit-bearers.

Paul's standard to them—"Let them eat their own bread"—is a standard not of selfishness but fruitfulness.

God laid down a similar standard through the prophet Isaiah:

> " . . . I am the Lord your God, who teaches you to profit. . . ."
>
> (Isaiah 48:17)

God expects us to bear fruit, in other words, by doing

things that benefit people around us. While the carnal man dreams of laying up riches so he can take life easy, the godly man dreams of serving the Lord every day of his life.

I once saw a series of drawings that brought this point home. The first frame showed an elderly woman sitting on her porch, knitting a sweater and babysitting a neighborhood child. The caption read, "You never retire from caring!"

The next panel showed an elderly man giving a quarter to a child who had lost his balloon. The caption read, "You never retire from sharing!"

The last panel showed an older woman talking on the telephone, making notes on a pad marked *Prayer Chain*. The caption read, "You never retire from praying."

That cartoonist's message was straight from the Word of God: You and I were made for a life of fruit-bearing, and we can judge whether our goals are godly by this important test.

I'm sure the Bible has many other acid tests for your goals, but let me mention one more: *A godly goal will be built on hope instead of despair.*

Many people have gloomy visions for the future. They see nothing but decline and destruction in the days ahead. They say the economy is going to collapse, the government is going to fold, the Russians are going to attack, and so on. These prognosticators of gloom have a goal of survival, nothing more.

But even when God's people are in trouble, He has hopeful goals for them. When the situation is grim, God's aim is gracious. While the Jews were being led away to bondage, for example, God gave the prophet Jeremiah a dream of hope. He told the Jews to settle down and prosper in Babylon, because He would bring them back to their homeland.

> "When seventy years have been completed for Babylon, I will visit you and fulfill My good word to you, to bring you back to this place. For I know the plans that I have for you," declares the Lord, "plans for welfare and not for calamity to give you a future and a hope."
>
> (Jeremiah 29:10-11)

It is difficult to imagine a worse situation than the Jews had. Their nation had been overrun by pagan hordes. Every citizen had lost his home. The temple had been destroyed. Their king had been humiliated. So God's message of hope in the midst of the smoldering ruins must have been electrifying!

Yet the Jews did not believe it. They listened to a false prophet named Shemaiah who said they should rebel against their conquerors and take the future into their own hands. Although God promised them a marvelous future, they lacked the faith to believe Him. I know of no place in Scripture where God predicts a gloomy future for His people. No matter how grave the situation, God has better things ahead for those who serve Him. Search the Scriptures if you think I'm exaggerating; see whether God's promises are gloomy or glorious. You will find in every case that God has "plans for welfare and not for calamity, to give you a future and a hope."

But sometimes that leads to a peculiar problem: Grand, incredible goals can also be scary. You may freeze with fear at the prospect of attempting to reach such goals, and you may get cold feet before taking the first step, much less the steps beyond. Does the Bible offer any assurances that you will achieve the goals you conceive?

In the next chapter we're going to deal with the fear of becoming a different person—the person God is calling you to be.

Before we do, let's review the three acid tests that you can apply to your goals to make sure they come from God:

1. Do they bring glory to God?

2. Do they bear fruit for God?

3. Are they built on hope instead of despair?

If your goals stand up to these tests, follow them, no matter how grand or incredible they seem to be. As the old prospectors learned, some things that glitter really *are* gold!

Go ahead and build your castles in the air. That's where they belong. Now put some foundations under them.
Henry David Thoreau

3

You *Can* Get There from Here

Grandfather Mountain is a beautiful landmark along the Appalachian Trail on the western edge of North Carolina where Dad and Mom often took our family. The mountain got its name from a craggy tower of rock that stands alone at the peak of the mountain, its weathered profile like the face of a wrinkled old man.

A wooden footbridge connects this peak to a nearby bluff where tourists can park and cross the wobbly swinging bridge to the Grandfather. My parents loved to do that. I didn't. Something about those creaking cables and undulating planks made my stomach uneasy. I watched dozens of people stride cheerfully across the bridge—even toddlers who held onto their mothers' hands. I watched my younger brother and sister cross the bridge and wave from the distant rock. But I never crossed. I was too scared.

Do you ever feel that way about your life's goals? Do you

hesitate to take the first step because you're not sure whether you can reach your goals? If so, let me share a secret: *A Christian can reach any goal God gives him if he stops asking, "What am I able to do?"*

Christians who lift their eyes to distant goals are apt to ask that question. They express a fear of the new, untried way of life that God calls them to walk. That fear can paralyze them, preventing them from taking even one step toward their goals. They feel as queasy as I did facing the bridge at Grandfather Mountain!

Perhaps you have that fear right now. Though we have not yet examined your life goals in detail, the very idea of becoming a different kind of person may be so unnerving that you would prefer to keep your feet firmly planted where you are.

But the Bible extends several promises to a goal-oriented Christian, assuring him that he *can* get there from here:

Promise #1:
God Knows the Way

You may not see how you could ever fulfill your goals, but God knows how you can. He has known from the beginning. The psalmist wrote,

> When my bones were being formed, carefully put together in my mother's womb, when I was growing there in secret, you knew that I was there—you saw me before I was born. The days allotted to me had all been recorded in your book, before any of them ever began.
>
> (Psalm 139:15-16, TEV)

Think about that for a moment: God saw you and me

from the very moment we were conceived, and He knew what our days would be. His purpose for our lives was laid before we were born. We may stumble into situations that seem to defeat the goals He has given us, but if His goals for us are perfect, then they must be attainable.

Almost every Christian has heard the story of Joni Eareckson Tada, who became paralyzed at age sixteen from a swimming accident. Many looked at Joni with pity, since she "could have done" so much with her life. Yet Joni has done much. She learned to draw by holding a pencil between her teeth. She's recorded several albums. She's begun a daily Christian radio program. She even has a new international ministry! Through all of these channels, she spreads the good news of Jesus Christ.

Joni and countless other Christians have proved Job 42:2, which says, "No purpose of Thine can be thwarted." Not one of God's purposes for you can be thwarted, either. Not by accident. Not by willful neglect. Not by *anything*. Your circumstances can never thwart God's ultimate purpose for your life.

But you can refuse to accept it. And there is a vast difference between following God's purpose or trying to buck it every step of the way. A vast difference in the satisfaction and the victory you find, not to mention in the sort of person you become.

Leslie Weatherhead, longtime pastor of City Temple in London, once said that the will of God is like a mountain stream: It is so small near its source that children can easily divert it with twigs and pebbles. Yet gravity still draws the stream of water down the mountainside. A stream can be delayed by huge hydroelectric dams but it cannot be stopped. It moves inexorably to the sea.

Likewise we may divert or delay the fulfillment of God's will, but we cannot destroy it. We can resist His claim upon our lives, but we cannot dismiss it. He calls us patiently toward the purpose He designed for us, and we are much happier when we understand that purpose, making it our own.

Promise #2:
God Reveals the Way

You may not have been willing to contemplate God's purpose for your life because you don't see how you can attain it. But Scripture says God will enable you to become any kind of person He wants you to become. Proverbs 16:3 promises:

Commit your works to the Lord, and your plans will be established.

This means we don't need to see every turn of life's maze before we step into it. We only need to trust the Guide who is leading us through. Though perplexing at first, the maze can even give us better understanding and maturity.

Archaeologists have unearthed an odd-looking hill in England. They thought at first it was a temple mound where Druids worshiped the sun, but they have found so many medieval artifacts that they now think it was a maze constructed by King Arthur as a testing ground for prospective knights.

Atop the hill was a stone tower surrounded by a labyrinth of hedges. A young man had to negotiate the thick maze of bushes in an allotted time. Then he had to brandish his sword against guards at the base of the tower, fight his way up the stairwell and claim a prize at the top. (A bag of gold? A beautiful girl? Your guess is as good as mine.)

The medieval ballads of England and France say that Merlin, the king's magician, divulged the route to lads he especially favored for the king's court. Only the fellows who got Merlin's help were able to reach the tower—and then they were on their own!

The way to your life goals may seem as perplexing as King Arthur's maze. You may feel mystified. But God has a way for you to reach the prize, and He will reveal that way to you as you step out. When you commit your works to the Lord, He will establish your plans.

Promise #3:
God Provides the Ability

In an age when some people put themselves down or make light of their own abilities, the Church has abetted this crime. One minister explained his technique for personal witnessing like this: "I've got to get a man lost before I can get him saved."

Too much Christian preaching and teaching has made unbelievers feel hopelessly lost, and believers that they are teetering on the brink of failure. Some pastors convey much good news about Christ but little good news about man. To be sure, the Bible recognizes human sin, immaturity and limitation. But it also shows we can rise above these things through the power of Christ. This is the part of the message we need to hear more.   Paul's Christian friends in Corinth, for example, were discouraged. False teachers were wrecking the church. Hedonistic culture in the city was drawing young people away from Christ. Church leaders practiced adultery and incest openly. Yet Paul began his letter to the Corinthians with this reminder:

Consider your calling, brethren, that there were

not many wise according to the flesh, not many mighty, not many noble; but God has chosen the foolish things of the world to shame the wise, and God has chosen the weak things of the world to shame the things which are strong, and the base things of the world and the despised, God has chosen, the things that are not, that He might nullify the things that are, that no man should boast before God.

(I Corinthians 1:26-29)

The Corinthian Christians were foolish, weak, base and despised, yet God chose them anyway! They lived, not in their power, but in His. That was the real measure of their ability.

In a later letter to his friends at Corinth, Paul confessed his own imperfections. In fact, he admitted a glaring imperfection that he called his "thorn in the flesh." But notice what he told the Corinthians about it:

. . . I entreated the Lord three times that it might depart from me. And He has said to me, "My grace is sufficient for you, for power is perfected in weakness." Most gladly, therefore, I will rather boast about my weaknesses, that the power of Christ may dwell in me.

(II Corinthians 12:8-9)

Think of it: The mighty power of God is best seen in a weak, imperfect, incapable life. That is not to say that a Christian should *remain* weak or imperfect! It means that God can take your life, inadequate though it seems, and mold it to His purpose. Although Paul felt a notable flaw in A.D. 60, we have no idea what it was, and we certainly don't think it hindered his mission.

Thus, I believe nothing is wasted in the Kingdom of God. Even the character traits that seem weak or cumbersome to us can be reclaimed and used to God's glory.

When we lived in Nashville, we drove past a huge scrapyard on our way to church—a mountain of rusty auto parts and bathtubs. The owners of that scrapyard crushed the salvage metal into tight, heavy bales, then loaded them onto flatcars for the steel mills in Birmingham, Alabama. There the scrap would be melted in white-hot furnaces to become ingots of pure metal once again.

I began to think of the scrapyard as my signpost to the church. Why not? The church is where God takes rusty, bent and broken lives and recycles them to suit His purpose. By ourselves we are nothing, but by His redeeming power we are perfect.

Think about your life goals once again. Don't consider your lack of ability, your weakness or your fear. Consider the God who chose you to be His. Consider the unlimited power of the One who ignited such brilliant dreams in your heart. Think about the life-changing grace of the God who calls you to become His man or woman.

You will begin to realize you *can* get there from here!

Salvation is free—"Jesus Paid It All." But the life of salvation is costly—"I Surrender All."

4

Building a Life
Will Cost You Plenty!

A young woman named Eugenia Price worked in Chicago as a radio scriptwriter. She received a generous salary and lived in a posh apartment. But she felt empty.

One weekend, visiting her parents in West Virginia, she met a high school friend named Ellen whom she had not seen for years. As they talked together, Eugenia perceived a radical difference in their lives. Although both had had a brash, arrogant attitude in high school, now Ellen had a quiet confidence, a radiant joy that fascinated Eugenia.

The trim businesswoman from Chicago asked her friend why she had changed. Ellen said it was because she had surrendered her life to Jesus Christ, and she urged Eugenia to do the same.

Over the next several months Ellen corresponded with Eugenia and pressed her to become a Christian. Finally

Eugenia could stand the pressure no more. She bought a train ticket to New York City, where Ellen worked in a soup kitchen run by an Episcopal church. She spent a full week with her, learning more about the Christian way of life.

Ellen kept saying, "Genie, if you're going to serve the Lord, you've got to serve Him one hundred percent. You've got to give Him everything."

That night as Eugenia was packing for the train trip back to Chicago, Ellen stopped by for a visit. Eugenia fussed with a cigarette as she told Ellen she was going to give Christianity a try.

"I really think you're far too radical about it," Eugenia laughed. "You say I'll have to give myself up entirely, and I think that's emotionalism on your part. Or dramatics." She had concluded that the Christian life could be enormous fun, and that Jesus didn't really require so much from her.

Ellen stood up from the couch, her eyes glinting with fire. "I didn't say that. Christ said it. It isn't my idea to give yourself up entirely. It's His."

The fact was, giving Christ everything didn't square with what Eugenia had learned about making a life for herself. She thought she had to carve her niche in the world, to make her own openings. So why give it all to Jesus? What if He decided to demolish the life she had made for herself and begin again with a different set of blueprints?

"Your interpretation is wrong," Eugenia sneered. "Extreme. Radical. God can adapt Himself to me more easily than I can adapt to Him!"

Gravely, Ellen picked up her coat to go. But before she did, she stepped over to Eugenia, so close that the electricity of the moment sparked between them.

"It won't work any other way," Ellen said. "Jesus says He is the way, the truth and the life; no man comes to the Father but by Him. He also says that if we try to save our lives, we'll lose them. But if we lose them for His sake we'll find them."

Eugenia sank down in a plush chair by the window. "Oh God, I wish I were dead!" she moaned.

"So do I," Ellen said.

Eugenia gasped.

"The most wonderful thing would be for the old Genie Price to die right now," continued Ellen, "so a new one could be born."

The headstrong writer from Chicago gazed out the window for a long moment. Her tears stopped flowing. With an uneasy smile she turned back to her friend.

"O.K.," she said. "I guess you're right."[1]

The bottom line for Eugenia Price was a total commitment to Christ. That was the only way she could start building a new life for God.

It's the only way anyone can start.

Let's take a look, then, at what Jesus said about selfsurrender. Let's try to understand how much He will require if you follow Him in pursuit of your life's goals. Jesus addressed this point specifically to a large crowd that was following Him:

> "If anyone comes to Me, and does not hate his own father and mother and wife and children and brothers and sisters, yes, and even his own life, he cannot be My disciple. Whoever does not carry his own cross and come after Me cannot be My disciple."
>
> (Luke 14:26-27)

Many people then wanted to follow Jesus. Whenever people see who Jesus really is, they want to follow Him. Many thousands have knelt at an altar and yearned for the wonderful changes He could bring to their lives. Many have promised to obey Him because they saw a marvelous transformation in the lives of others who obeyed Him.

Unfortunately, many of these Christians deserved the label some sociologists have given the 1970s—the "Me Decade," when people placed a premium on personal satisfaction. Throngs of people claimed to be born again because it felt good to be cleansed of guilt and sin and to belong to a supportive group of other born-again people.

Yet Christ does not leave the stars in our eyes. He soon confronts us with the cost of following Him. The feeling-oriented disciples of the '70s followed Jesus as long as it felt good, but eventually they learned that the Christian life isn't always warm and cozy. Sacrifice, self-denial, suffering—these are also part of the Christian life. And many exuberant Christians have turned away from Christ when the good feelings ebbed away.

Jesus knew this would happen with the people who gladly listened to His parables of the Kingdom. So He warned the crowd of the cost of following Him. And He warns you and me as well.

Before we focus on specific goals God has for our lives, we must be sure to count the cost of fulfilling them.

Holy Hate

When Jesus said that anyone who came to Him had to hate his father and mother and wife and children and brothers and sisters and even his own life, He did not mean by the word *hate* what we usually associate with it. When you or I say we "hate" something, we mean that we want to put it away from us; we reject it.

Jesus did not mean here for us to reject our families. That would contradict everything else Jesus taught about the family. He used the word *hate* to imply that we be willing to let these things go. Love embraces; hate releases. So the word *hate* is the opposite of being attached.

We might paraphrase Jesus' statement like this: "If anyone comes to Me and is not willing *to let go* of his family . . . even his own life, he cannot be My disciple."

Such a price is higher than some people are willing to pay. They think there might be an easier way to be happy, a less demanding discipline that would please God, a more "flexible" commitment to make. So they shop around. They try substitute gospels. They experiment with religious-sounding forms of pop psychology.

But nothing can take the place of full commitment to Jesus Christ. Nothing else can raise us to full stature before God. Nothing else can make us children of God and eternal heirs with Christ. Only in the red-hot crucible of commitment can we discover the refined gold of God's blessing.

Other people think, "Why count the cost of following Jesus? Why not toss caution to the winds and commit my life to Him?" That approach sounds noble until God asks them for something they never expected to give. Then they are forced to take stock of their commitment. In the broiling heat of crisis, they wonder whether they should have given Christ a blank check with their lives. It seems He wants to draw too much from their account, and they wonder if they were a bit too hasty.

That is why Jesus warned us to count the cost of discipleship at the outset. Before the demands come, before our commitment is tested, before He drafts our blank check, we should consider how much we are willing to give Him in the line of duty.

To help us do this, Jesus painted two pictures.

First, He described a stonemason who planned to build a tower. "Which one of you," asked Jesus, "when he wants to build a tower, does not first sit down and calculate the cost, to see if he has enough to complete it?" (Luke 14:28).

Unfortunately, not everyone does this. I have passed what was supposed to be a motel near the town of Marion, Indiana. I am sure the developers envisioned it to be a beautiful facility. The cinderblocks are in place. Some of the plumbing is installed. Even some brickwork was started. But the developers ran out of money and couldn't finish the job. So travelers pass the half-built shell and wag their heads in dismay. What a waste of resources!

A builder should accurately count his costs before he starts to build. And so should a disciple of Jesus.

The second picture Jesus painted was that of a king. "What king," He asked, "when he sets out to meet another king in battle, will not first sit down and take counsel whether he is strong enough . . . ?" (Luke 14:31).

A commander should know how many troops are at his command as well as how many the adversary has. Yet how often human pride overrides this simple logic. A tragic miscalculation brought on the Falkland Islands crisis in 1982. The generals of Argentina had fewer soldiers, boats or planes than Great Britain; yet they assumed the British would not try to defend this frigid island outpost. So they sent a landing party to stake their claim on the Falklands. They ran the risk of battle and they lost. Hundreds of lives were lost because the generals failed to count the cost realistically.

Likewise, no Christian should dare tangle with the enemy of his soul until he has counted the cost of arming himself. The Bible says our enemy "prowls about like a roaring lion, seeking someone to devour" (I Peter 5:8). We may be destroyed if we charge into the battle unprepared!

These two word pictures from Jesus remind us of how important it is to count the cost of discipleship. This is not a trivial exercise. We must know how much we are willing to lay on the line for His sake *before* it is required of us.

The Bottom Line

Accountants like to talk about the "bottom line" of a balance sheet. After all their mathematical turns, it comes down to this: Did we break even? Were we able to meet our expenses?

Jesus tallies the bottom line of a Christian's commitment in clear, concrete terms. He says we must be willing to lose our family, possessions, even our life if we intend to be His disciple.

How much will it cost to serve the Lord? Everything! You can't become God's man or woman by investing ten percent of what you have, or fifty percent, or even eighty percent. Someday He will ask you for the rest. "No one can be My disciple," Jesus said, "unless he is willing to give up *all.*"

That could mean one of two things. It could mean that God will take everything from you. Sometimes He does that, removing money, property, family or even health to help you fulfill the mission He gives you.

It could mean, on the other hand, that He will leave everything in your possession and expect you to use all of it for His purposes. More often God works this way, calling you to manage what you have for His glory.

Joyce Landorf was a talented Christian singer and much-sought lecturer for women's groups. She traveled widely in her native state of California. Then a rare disease attacked the hinge of her jaw, so that she felt extreme pain whenever she spoke. Her physician recommended complete rest.

Joyce sat at home in self-pity while her husband continued his fine ministry at a Christian college. What could she do? God seemed to have taken away her only ability for serving Him. It didn't seem fair!

But Joyce learned much about God in those months of silence. She learned that her voice really did belong to God. She had stated this blithely before dozens of audiences; but now she knew it was true. Her voice was His to use—or remove. During that painful convalescence, she felt the full impact of Psalm 46:10: "Be still and know that I am God. . . (KJV)."

Joyce Landorf was able to speak and sing in public again. But during her divinely imposed silence she learned to write Christian articles and books. God suspended the use of one gift so that she would learn to employ others. And one of the first manuscripts from her typewriter was a book entitled, *The High Cost of Growing.*[2]

Sooner or later every Christian learns the high cost of serving God. Jesus said we should count the cost because building a life will cost us plenty—that is to say, *everything*. But weigh that cost against the privilege of serving Him.

Notes

[1] Eugenia Price, *The Burden Is Light!* (Old Tappan, N.J.: Spire Books, 1966), chapter 17.

[2] Joyce Landorf, *The High Cost of Growing* (Nashville: Thomas Nelson, 1978). Now retitled, *I'm Still Growing.*

Modern symbols of achievement—a stopwatch, a runner and a tape.
Jesus' symbols of achievement—a seed, a stalk and a breadloaf.
(Cf. Mark 4:26-29; Matthew 13:33)

5

Are You on Schedule?

The town of Littleburg had a problem: Its train was always late. Only one train rumbled into town each day, but the exasperated passengers waiting on the platform knew it would be at least a half-hour late, maybe more.

One bright autumn afternoon, the stationmaster noticed a black plume of engine smoke just beyond the hill. He checked his pocketwatch. How could it be? The train was on time today! He grabbed the phone and dialed the operator (Littleburg's equivalent of the Distant Early Warning System) and told her the astonishing news.

In moments, the mayor came roaring up to the station in a police car. The schoolbell rang and children poured out into the street to welcome the train. A long yellow bus jostled into the station's parking lot and disgorged the local high school band for an impromptu salute. This was a historic day! At last the train was on schedule.

As the engine ground to a halt and the mayor straightened his tie, getting ready to make a speech, the engineer peered out of the cab. "What's all the fuss about?" he asked.

"Why, surely you know!" the mayor laughed. "We've come to congratulate you for bringing in the train on time!"

The engineer swallowed hard. "Well, I hate to disappoint you folks," he said. "But, you see . . . this is yesterday's train!"

Schedules. We grumble because of them. We say we hate them. But we Americans are notorious clock-watchers and calendarmarkers. And that's not altogether bad!

Schedules help us accomplish things we really want to do. The schedule at your shop or office allows you to work at definite, regular hours and still have time for personal activities. The bus schedule allows children to have dependable transportation to school. The garbage pick-up schedule allows you to set those bulging plastic bags at your curb on a given night and know they will be gone in the morning. Complain about them if you wish. But your life would be more frustrating without schedules than with them.

Most of us seem to have a sense of timing in the vocational decisions we make, too. We use phrases like these:

"I knew the time was right to. . . ."

"I had arrived at the stage of life when. . . ."

"God showed me I was ready to. . . ."

I hear a sense of timing in our comments about the reasons for abandoning certain vocations, too. We say:

"I wasn't moving fast enough."

"It was a dead-end job."

"I should have been much farther along."

Obviously we set goals with a sense of timing and scheduling, as well as with a sense of purpose and destination. But do we know God's schedule? Does God indeed *have* a schedule? Or are we just following a subconscious sense of timing, instilled by our culture and upbringing?

The Schedule for Jesus' Life

To get a handle on these questions, let's take a look at Jesus' sense of timing. The four Gospels indicate that Jesus was following a divine schedule in His ministry.

The fourth Gospel records, for example, that in the second year of Jesus' public ministry, He was "unwilling to walk in Judea, because the Jews were seeking to kill Him" (John 7:1). Jesus told His disciples to go up to Jerusalem to celebrate the Passover without Him. When His brothers (that is, His half-brothers born to Jesus' mother, Mary) tried to urge Him on, to make a public display of His works, Jesus still refused. Pay careful attention to His reply:

> "My time is not yet at hand, but your time is always opportune. The world cannot hate you; but it hates Me because I testify of it, that its deeds are evil. Go up to the feast yourselves; I do not go up to this feast because My time has not yet fully come."
>
> (John 7:6-8)

John records that after His half-brothers left, the Lord did go to Jerusalem secretly. So why did Jesus say His time was "not yet fully come" to attend the Passover?

Apparently He meant that the time was not right for Him to enter the city publicly as the Messiah, thereby forcing the Jewish leaders to deal with Him.

He also went back to Jerusalem to celebrate Passover the next year. But on that occasion, He said, "The hour has come for the Son of Man to be glorified" (John 12:23). This time Jesus entered the city publicly with a great deal of fanfare, receiving the glorification of mankind. But He also died on the cross and His heavenly Father raised Him from the dead; so He received the glorification of God as well.

Jesus had known He would force a confrontation with the Jewish leaders when He entered Jerusalem with His relatives, friends and admirers cheering Him on. This may be why He stated in John 7 that His time had "not yet fully come." But in John 12, when He declared, "The hour has come," He entered the city publicly, coming to grips with the consequences.

It is interesting, in light of Jesus' keen awareness of timing, that He could chafe at schedules, too. His goals were to be the compassionate Teacher, crucified Messiah and risen Lord. But in the last days of His ministry, Jesus sounded almost impatient to accomplish these goals:

> "I have come to cast fire upon the earth; and how I wish it were already kindled! But I have a baptism to undergo, and how distressed I am until it is accomplished!"
>
> (Luke 12:49-50)

Not only did Jesus seem in some sense to be chafing at His schedule; but I find two other vital insights here. First, that Jesus sensed God had a schedule for His life, and second, that Jesus measured His schedule in *fulfilled* time.

Another Way to Measure Time

All of us know how to measure elapsed time. Whenever we glance at a wristwatch or tear a leaf from a desk calendar, we note the passing of time. We assume that every day is like every other day in this respect. This kind of time measurement is neat, orderly and predictable. We tend to think of it as the only way to measure time.

But there is another way. The Bible calls it *fulfilled* time. The New Testament says that God acts in "the fullness of time" to accomplish every facet of His will (e.g., Romans 11:25; Galatians 4:4; Ephesians 1:10).

This may help to explain why Jesus would not give His disciples an exact date for His return. He said that "of that day and hour no one knows, not even the angels of heaven, nor the Son" (Matthew 24:36).

Perhaps there is no set date anyway, since it depends on the fulfillment of certain things. (I'm speculating at this point, of course. But if God planned other events according to fulfilled time, might He not do the same in deciding when to send His Son back to earth?)

Life may be measured more reliably in fulfilled time, as we saw in Jesus' experience. When Jesus said His time to enter Jerusalem was "not yet fulfilled," He was not watching a calendar or checking a celestial datebook. He knew when conditions were right for Him to enter the next phase of His ministry.

Let me try to illustrate the idea of fulfilled time vs. elapsed time with a practical, everyday example. Imagine you are roasting a turkey for Thanksgiving dinner. You can time the cooking cycle in two ways—with a clock or with a thermometer.

The wrapper on the turkey may tell you to cook it at 350 degrees, allowing 45 minutes for each pound of the turkey's weight. So you multiply the formula and set your stove clock accordingly. This is the elapsed time method. About halfway through the telecast of the Macy's Parade, you hear the buzzer go off. So you pull the roasting pan from the oven and serve your golden brown delicacy. Perfect every time, right?

Wrong. Any number of factors might change the cooking time required. The turkey may not have been completely thawed. The oven may not be as hot as your control says it is. The pan may not be the recommended distance from the coil. When the recommended time has elapsed, your turkey might be a bit rare—or burned!—depending on all of these factors.

So you learn to measure time with a thermometer. You consult your cookbook, which has a table of temperatures for roasting. It says that when the temperature inside your turkey reaches a certain point it is fully cooked, regardless of how much time has elapsed. So you insert a meat thermometer into the bird, pop it into the oven, and check the gauge now and then to see when the cooking is done. This is the fulfilled time system. When proper conditions are met, you turn off your oven and serve the turkey.

Considering all the factors involved, fulfilled time is a more reliable measure than elapsed time.

How to Know When Your Time Is "Fulfilled"

Jesus' ministry leads us, then, to two important conclusions: First, that God has a pattern or schedule for His servants; and second, that God's servants can discern that schedule if they mark the fullness of time rather than the simple passage of time.

How can you do that, ensuring that the conditions are right for you to take the next step in fulfilling your life's goals? I believe maturity is the key. When you are spiritually mature for your stage of life, you may consider taking a further step toward your goals.

Maturity is a measurement that applies differently to different people. A mature infant will gurgle and coo, while a mature high school student will recite the Gettysburg Address. They are vastly different in their capabilities, yet each is mature.

So how do you measure spiritual maturity? Here are some guidelines:

1. *You are making the most of the opportunities God has given you.* To get a picture of what this means, review Jesus' Parable of the Talents (Matthew 25:14-30).

2. *Your life is bringing glory to God.* This means your life acts as a mirror, reflecting God's blessings to people who have not seen what He can do (Matthew 5:14-16).

3. *You can discriminate between good and evil choices.* You have learned the difference by repeatedly choosing the good (see Hebrews 5:14).

4. *You gladly receive instruction from God's Word and act upon it.* You have become "good soil" for the seed of the Word (Luke 8:4-15).

5. *You measure yourself by Christ.* He is the true model of spiritual maturity, rather than your friends or

famous Christians you have read about (Ephesians 4:13).

6. *You think as an adult*—that is, as a spiritual "adult" (I Corinthians 12:20). Psychologists have noted the following characteristics of adult thinking:

   a. Acknowledges reality. Confronts the true facts of each situation, even when the facts are painful.
   b. Defers satisfaction. Willing to wait months, even years, for the things desired.
   c. Contributes to community. Addresses the needs of neighbors as well as personal needs.
   d. Concedes predominance. Knows one cannot get his own way every time.

Is your own thinking mature in each of these respects?

7. *You care for others as deeply as you care for yourself.* This may seem like a restatement of characteristic "c" in the list above, but there is a vital difference: The psychologically mature person usually may address his neighbor's needs after his own needs are satisfied. The spiritually mature person often deals with his neighbor's needs *before* he deals with his own (Philippians 2:3-4).

8. *You apply what you've learned from your failures.* This is a rich concept. When you have a disheartening experience, don't write it off as a failure; consider it an experiment. Remember that an experiment never fails. It always teaches you something.

Dr. Malcolm Rigel, who teaches counseling at Warner Southern College in Lake Wales, Florida, gave me an interesting sidelight on this. We were returning from lunch one day when I said, "Mac, I appreciate the way you help people deal with their failures. You've brought up the subject of failure in a couple of retreats I've attended. You seem to have a much more positive attitude about it than I have."

He grinned. "Joe, the compost pile is the richest part of my garden. That's where I throw my kitchen scraps, lawn clippings, and all the manure I can find. It's a smelly, repulsive-looking thing. But the compost pile decays into rich humus that will feed my garden next spring. My failures and disappointments are like that. They trouble me. I would like to ignore them. But I've learned that failures can provide rich compost for my life if I apply what I learn from them."

What have you learned from your "experiments"? How have you used the compost of your life? Your answers will indicate your level of maturity.

God does have a schedule for your life, a plan for becoming the person He expects you to be. But He measures your progress by the signs of spiritual maturity in your life, rather than by the days marked off your desk calendar. Here is a summary of those guidelines of spiritual maturity. Use it as a checklist when you wonder if you are on schedule with God's will:

Marks of a Mature Life
(or, *How to Know When You've Fulfilled God's Goals for This Phase of Your Life*)

1. You make the most of the opportunities God has given you.
2. Your life brings glory to God.

3. You discriminate between good and evil choices.

4. You receive instruction from God's Word and act upon it.

5. You measure yourself by Christ.

6. You think as an adult.

7. You care for others as deeply as you care for yourself.

8. You apply what you have learned from your failures.

*In many areas of life, God invites us to
consult our own sanctified preferences.*
Paul E. Little[1]

6

Setting Goals:
A Portrait of Your Dream

Gatlinburg, Tennessee, is a tourist town at the entrance
to the Great Smoky Mountains National Park. Novelty
shops and restaurants are jammed side-by-side along the
streets. While I strolled along the main street of Gatlinburg one crisp October afternoon, I found a portrait
painter outside a candy shop sketching the figure of a
young man from a color snapshot. Her technique taught
me a lot, not only about portrait-painting but about goal-
setting.

First she took a broad brush and swabbed a faint tan
color across the entire canvas. Then she marked the center point with a fine-tipped brush. (I understand that some
portrait painters sketch a grid across the entire canvas, like
a schoolboy's graph paper.) This is called *staining and
marking* the canvas.

The artist then outlined the dimensions and orientation

of her subject. The snapshot showed him in a quarter-turn pose, but she turned him to a more dramatic profile position, using the fine-tipped brush to outline the bust of this handsome young man.

Next she sketched the *features* of her subject's face. I could see the distinctive qualities of his personality begin to emerge. Every line and crinkle expressed something of the young man's identity. The artist accentuated features only suggested by the photo; she reinterpreted the photo to express the character she saw in this youthful figure.

The Gatlinburg artist deftly portrayed her subject's expression. What was the young man's habitual mood? His outlook? His attitude toward life? I could sense each of these as she deepened the shadows here and there, lifted the highlights and gave just the right touch to his eyes and mouth. She seemed to have a knack for expressing his character, which is the true genius of portrait-painting—the quality that sets a portrait apart from a photograph.

Then the sidewalk painter roughed in the *background* of her portrait. She surrounded the subject with things that indicated his special interests and involvements. Although the snapshot showed him in a plaid sports shirt, she clothed him in a soldier's uniform and put the Marine Corps insignia in the background. Glancing at some other canvases, I saw the portrait of another young man in which she had placed a slide rule and blueprints, suggesting that he was an architect. She was able to express a great deal about her subject in the surrounding details.

My art lesson in Gatlinburg also taught me some things about setting goals for my life, things that might help you, too. A portrait painter and a goal-setter are doing essentially the same thing. A portrait painter expresses an image in her mind. When I set goals, I tangibly express the dream in my mind. Our tools are different but our purpose is the same. Both of us want to frame that mental picture so we can refer to it again and again.

Let's review the portrait painter's work and see what we can learn about setting goals for our lives.

Staining, Marking and Outlining

When the sidewalk painter stained and marked her canvas, she determined what the overall mood of the portrait would be. The subtle tan color gave the finished portrait a quiet, dignified atmosphere. When Leonardo da Vinci painted "The Last Supper" on a monastery wall in Milan, he began by painting the whole wall with a snowy white primer, so that in the finished painting, the somber brown tones of Christ and the Twelve stand in sharp relief against the bright white sky outside.

The staining and marking of the painter's canvas are like God's underlying presence in your life. His presence will determine the mood of your entire life. Your vocation, marital status, family makeup, and other things are the details of the picture; but your relationship with God determines the nature of your personal picture, now and in the future.

When you dream about your life ten years from now, how do you see your relationship with God? Here are some statements that will help you describe the relationship as you envision it:

1. I will most often see God
   ____ as a gentle Shepherd.
   ____ a compassionate Friend.
   ____ a wise Teacher.
   ____ a righteous Judge.

2. I believe that my relationship with God will be

_____ deeper.

_____ as it is now.

_____ shallower.

3. I believe He will reveal His will to me most often through

_____ Scripture.

_____ inner guidance by the Holy Spirit.

_____ the counsel of godly friends.

4. I will come to worship services with an attitude of

_____ joy and expectancy.

_____ awe and wonder.

_____ solemnity and reverence.

_____ fear and hesitation.

5. I believe God will require

_____ no significant changes in my lifestyle.

_____ a few minor changes in my lifestyle.

_____ radical changes in my lifestyle. Describe:

6. I believe He will call me to work in

_____ a culture familiar to me.

_____ a culture foreign to me.

7. I believe I will share my convictions

_____ only when asked.

_____ quietly and respectfully.

_____ openly and aggressively.

8. I believe He will use me in my neighborhood as a

_____ companion and helper.

_____ concerned listener.

_____ defender of people's rights.

_____ proclaimer of the truth.

9. I believe He will use me in the church as a

_____ deacon (who provides for people's material

_____ needs).
_____ priest (who listens and heals).
_____ ruler (who directs and instructs).
_____ prophet (who speaks and challenges).

10. I believe the Lord will use me most effectively by
    _____ what I am.
    _____ what I do.
    _____ what I say.

11. My attitude toward His will is going to be
    _____ cheerful acceptance.
    _____ reluctant cooperation.
    _____ complaining resistance.

12. When I consider God's purpose for my life, I feel
    _____ overwhelmed.
    _____ uneasy.
    _____ comfortable.
    _____ challenged.
    Explain _why_ you feel as you do:

13. When I consider who I am today, I feel
    _____ restless, wanting to become as I once was.
    _____ satisfied and contented.
    _____ restless, wanting to become a new person.

Features

The next step of the artist's work was to sketch in the features of the young man's face. She began to express the personality of her subject.

I've enjoyed looking at some of the self-portraits made by the great Dutch painter, Rembrandt. I can see a change in the features of Rembrandt's face as the years went by. The relaxed, confident expression of his youth gave way to troubled, weary lines in his old age; he was plagued by family problems and debt, which took their toll on his character.

I wonder what your character lines will be ten or twenty years from now. What will be the distinctive marks of your personality? Here are some statements that will help you express what you see:

1. I believe I will be
   _____ an introverted person.
   _____ an outgoing person.

2. I believe my attitude toward strangers will be
   _____ distrustful.
   _____ trustful.

3. I believe my attitude toward my family will be
   _____ loving.
   _____ resentful.

4. I believe my view of the future will be
   _____ confident.
   _____ expectant.
   _____ hopeful.
   _____ gloomy.

5. I believe my sense of humor will be
   _____ gentle and warm.
   _____ rollicking and boisterous.
   _____ sarcastic.

6. I believe I will cry
   _____ when I feel grieved or disappointed.
   _____ when I feel angry or sorrowful.
   _____ when I feel ridiculed or embarrassed.
   _____ hardly ever.

7. I will have the most difficulty controlling my

_____ sorrow.
_____ regret.
_____ fear.
_____ impulsiveness.
_____ anger.

Background

The Gatlinburg painter embellished her portraits with symbols of the subject's life, such as military insignia or tools of the trade. She put her subject in suitable clothes and planted him in surroundings that told us something about his identity.

Background details can express the personality of the subject as revealingly as the set of his lips or the lines on his brow. Who can forget Winslow Homer's dynamic paintings of sailors and fishermen straining against their ship rigging as they peer out from the soggy hoods of their rain slickers? Or what would we know about the farm couple in Grant Wood's "American Gothic" without the man's bib overalls and pitchfork, the woman's apron, and the white clapboard farmhouse behind them?

Who will be the people in the background of your life ten years from now? How will you get along with them? What will be your style of living?

Here are some statements to help you describe the background details of your dreams for the future:

1. I believe my co-workers will be
   _____ searching for answers.
   _____ confident they have all the answers.

2. When I'm in a large group of people, I will be
   _____ a quiet spectator.
   _____ a lively spectator.

_____ a quiet participant.
_____ a lively participant.
_____ the focus of attention.

3. When I become the kind of person God wants me to be, I may have trouble getting along with
_____ other Christians who don't believe as I do.
_____ uncommitted people.
_____ skeptics.

4. I believe that when my family sees the Lord's purpose for my life, they will
_____ approve and encourage me.
_____ approve but not give much encouragement.
_____ disapprove but not try to discourage me.
_____ disapprove and try to discourage me.

5. I think I will feel uncomfortable with
_____ quiet people.
_____ talkative people.

6. I think I will feel most comfortable with
_____ people who are a lot like me.
_____ people who are different from me.

7. I believe that other people's approval will
_____ mean a great deal to me.
_____ concern me but not guide me.
_____ make no difference to me.

8. My life would be changed the most by the death of _____, for these reasons:

9. The person I am most eager to spend the future with is _____, because:

10. I believe I will have completed this level of education:

_____ elementary school.
_____ high school.
_____ vocational school or junior college.
_____ bachelor's degree.
_____ master's or doctor's degree.

11. I believe my annual income ten years from now will be
_____ less than $10,000.
_____ $10,000 to $25,000.
_____ over $25,000 but less than $75,000.
_____ over $75,000.

12. I believe I will be reading books on these subjects:

13. I believe I will attend meetings of civic groups, social clubs or church groups such as these:

14. My house/condominium/apartment will be located in
_____ the city.
_____ the suburbs.
_____ the country.

15. I believe I will be living in
_____ the Northeast.
_____ the Midwest.
_____ the South.
_____ the West.
_____ elsewhere (name area of the world:)

These last few questions may seem trivial, but they will help you complete the portrait of your future self.

You now have a full picture of your desires for the future. You have portrayed your goals; you have described yourself as you expect to be.

You can summarize your goals by compiling sentences with a component from each section of questions. You might say, for example, "The Lord will use me most effectively by what I do; my sense of humor will be rollicking and boisterous; and my attitude toward strangers will be trustful." Or you might say, "The Lord will use me most effectively by what I am; my co-workers will be people searching for answers; and my view of the future will be expectant."

Each time you compose a sentence like this, you get a thumbnail sketch of what you anticipate for your life; you get a statement of your goals.

Testing Your Goals

Test these goals with the same biblical standards we discussed earlier for testing dreams. Then ask yourself some questions:

Do I have any wrong goals? Do any of my goals miss the mark of what God expects from one of His children? There is nothing virtuous, for example, about a person who always resents or distrusts other people.

Do I have any inadequate goals? Have I scaled down my God-given dream to fit my own shortcomings? You may hesitate to commit yourself to your God-given goals because you don't have the proper gift or ability, but God can provide these, as we will see.

Do I have any outmoded goals? Am I clinging to a life-style that once was right for me but no longer honors the Lord? You may have lived in a four-bedroom home in your child-rearing years, but now the children have grown up and moved away from home and your lifestyle ought to change.

Are these really my goals, or am I adopting someone

else's goals in order to please them? Well-meaning relatives or friends can easily impose their goals upon you. They say, "You ought to be a cartographer like your Uncle Ed," or, "You have a knack for working with children." With countless good suggestions and helpful hints, they construct their own portraits of what they feel you ought to be. And it may be far easier to accept their ready-made dreams than to articulate your own.

The psychologist Theodore Lidz tells the story of a young man whose father expected him to become a building contractor. The father had made a lucrative business of it, so he thought his son should continue the family tradition. The son didn't like the construction business; he wanted to be a concert pianist. But to please his father, he went to trade school and acquired the necessary skills. Then he built a sprawling apartment complex in New York City and sold it at a large profit. His father was very happy—until the young man took his profits and went to Europe to study piano!

The young millionaire had decided to pursue his own goals rather than his dad's. I don't know whether his father ever forgave him; but the young man knew he could not be accountable to his father forever.[2]

To serve God, you must be accountable to Him. You must live in a way that pleases and glorifies Him. Other people will clamor for satisfaction, but if you are striving to please God, you cannot please all of them. How about it—can you give a good account of yourself to God?

Visions can be wonderful. God-given visions can become challenging goals. Let's be sure our visions and goals come from Him. If we plan to build on a framework of faulty goals, we are sure to be disappointed. But if we build on goals that honor the Lord, our lives will be rewarding and satisfying.

Planning to build—that's the next step.

Notes

[1] Paul E. Little, *Affirming the Will of God* (Downers Grove, Ill.: InterVarsity Press, 1971), p. 7.

[2] Theodore Lidz, *The Person* (New York: Basic Books, 1976), p. 490.

We can be sure that any job, marriage, move, investment, or expenditure which leads us away from being a communicator of the Lord is not best for us or His purposes in our lives.

Lloyd J. Ogilvie[1]

7

Making Plans:

Becoming What You Choose

Terrence Johnston works one of the last one-man coal-mining operations in this country. In a low, dusty tunnel shaft near Altoona, Pennsylvania, he burrows chunks of soft coal from the earth with a pickax. Two Shetland ponies, harnessed to an oak dump car, stand obediently behind him. On a good day they might haul two tons of coal from the tunnel. Terrence sells it to his neighbors for $25 a ton, with $10 of that going to taxes and lease rights. He lives with his wife and two daughters in a tarpaper shack at the mouth of the mine.

"It's nothing to brag about," says Terrence, "but it's good enough for me. Some people are dissatisfied with their work. Me, I'm perfectly comfortable and quite content. I'm here by choice, and I'm just as happy as if I had good sense."[2]

Frankly, his comment proves he already has good sense. By affirming that he is there by choice, Terrence Johnston shows a profound insight that many philosophers never reveal. You and I got where we are by choice. We will be where we are ten years hence by choice. And so it will be forever.

God lets every person choose how he will live. God could be sovereign in all things, but He allows man to be sovereign in the power of choosing.

Man chooses how he will live in spite of circumstances. Circumstances limited the work of John Bunyan, the eloquent Nonconformist preacher of seventeenth-century England, when the authorities jailed him and banned his preaching. But Bunyan could still choose how to live in jail; no man could take that away from him. So Bunyan wrote *Pilgrim's Progress* and other classic devotional books while sitting on the dank, musty straw of his cell. He chose how he would live in spite of his circumstances.

Grim consequences faced Chester Bitterman and other Wycliffe Bible translators in the jungles of Central America. They knew they might be captured, tortured and killed by rebel soldiers in the area. Bitterman considered the consequences and chose to go anyway. He was kidnapped, accused of being a spy, and shot. Chet Bitterman chose how he would live in spite of the consequences.

A person also chooses how he will live in spite of coercion. Communist coercion has filled the prison camps of Russia with hundreds of Christians arrested for distributing gospel literature and meeting for worship. In many cases, the Soviet government stripped these people of their jobs and confiscated their possessions in an attempt to pressure them into giving up their faith. Yet these Christians chose nevertheless to evangelize their country.

No one can say he is unable to make choices. God gives every man and woman the power to choose. We may have to choose in the shadow of unfavorable circumstances or unexpected coercion; but every one of us chooses what he will do.

A goal-oriented Christian chooses to live according to God's general will and according to the unique pattern God has established for him. These daily choices are the plans of his life.

In the first six chapters, we focused on our future vision of ourselves—our dreams—which are in essence our goals. We have articulated them. We have tested them. We have corrected them where they would dishonor the Lord or betray our integrity. Now we are ready to make plans for achieving our goals, so we can become what we have chosen.

Examples of Goal-Oriented Plans

Let's look at samples of plans that might be used to achieve the goals set in Chapter 6. We'll refine these plans later; for now, I just want to give you an idea of how effective, goal oriented plans would look:

Goal	*Plan*
1. A deeper relationship with God	1. Spend half-an-hour in private prayer each morning; read one chapter of the New Testament each day.

2. An outgoing person	2. Introduce myself to one stranger each day; learn his/her name and occupation; send a friendship greeting card.
3. Graduation from vocational training school	3. Get catalog from Ivy Tech; schedule interview with admissions director.

There are three important features to observe in these goal-oriented plans.

First, notice that each of the goals is a "be" statement. Even #3, which seems at first to be a "do" statement, is really saying, "I will *be* a vocational school graduate." Each "do" statement is a specific plan of action that moves you one step closer to becoming the person God expects you to be.

Second, notice that each plan statement is a specific plan. We tend to make vague, general plans so we won't have to admit failure. We can say, for example, "Oh, I *did* take more time for Bible study last week, like that morning I read the Lord's Prayer at breakfast." A vague plan cannot fail, because it allows us to define later what the plan really was. By the same token, a vague plan seldom motivates us to make significant change in our lives. If you want to reach specific life goals, you need to make specific plans.

Third, notice that the plans are only beginning steps; they would not renovate a person's life overnight. We should always think in terms of long-range growth. We acquired our present habits, attitudes and intentions over many years, so we should expect to change them over many years. We need to allow a realistic amount of time for achieving our goals.

Counselors at weight-loss clinics say that people who set unrealistic goals or plans are usually the ones who drop out. There is the desperate high school senior, for example, who wants to shed two dress sizes before the prom. In order to lose thirty pounds by the end of the month, she goes on a crash diet—500 calories a day. She is setting herself up for failure, because the human body cannot handle such radical changes in such a short time. The same is true for any other aspect of life.

When the Bible says you can be "transformed by the renewing of your mind" (Romans 12:2), it does not mean you can be transformed as soon as you change your mind! Just as the high school senior needs to change her pattern of eating, and lose her thirty pounds in a more gradual, permanent way, so God takes a while to change your life. He must redirect your heart, your heart must redirect your mental outlook, and your mental outlook must redirect your actions.

So be patient with yourself. As the Indiana philosopher Max Ehrmann wrote, "Enjoy your achievements as well as your plans."[3]

Your plans should be aimed at action; they should be specific; and they should allow realistic time for change. With these guidelines in mind, let's begin making some plans for your life based on the goals you have set.

Worksheet for Planning

Here is a simple method you can use to make plans for reaching your life goals, a method you can employ any time you believe the time is ripe for a change in your life:

A. Compare your real self to your ideal self.

Check the appropriate slot on each of the scales that follow. First, put an X for each of the answers you gave in

Chapter 6 for your future, ideal self. Then put an O to show where you think you are now. Here is a sample:

1. I will most often see God as

    ☒ Shepherd ☐ Friend ◙ Teacher ☐ Judge

This person ideally wants to see God as a gentle Shepherd (X), but right now sees Him as a wise Teacher (O). The person will need to make changes in this area to become more like his ideal self.

Now that you see how the scales work, fill in the X's and O's:

Your Relationship with God

1. I will most often see God as

    ☐ Shepherd ☐ Friend ☐ Teacher ☐ Judge

2. I believe my relationship with God will be

    ☐ deeper ☐ as it is (was) ☐ shallower

3. I believe He will reveal His will to me most often through

    ☐ Scripture ☐ Spirit ☐ counsel

4. I will come to worship services with an attitude of

    ☐ joy ☐ awe ☐ solemnity ☐ fear

5. I believe God will require (has required)

    ☐ no changes ☐ few changes ☐ radical changes in my
                                               lifestyle

6. I believe He will call (has called) me to work in

☐ familiar culture ☐ foreign culture

7. I believe I will share my convictions

☐ when asked ☐ quietly ☐ openly

8. I believe He will use me in my neighborhood as a

☐ companion ☐ listener ☐ defender ☐ proclaimer

9. I believe He will use me in the church as a

☐ deacon ☐ priest ☐ ruler ☐ prophet

10. I believe God will use me most effectively by

☐ what I am ☐ what I do ☐ what I say

11. My attitude toward His will is going to be

☐ acceptance ☐ cooperation ☐ resistance

12. When I consider God's purpose for my life, I feel

☐ overwhelmed ☐ uneasy ☐ comfortable ☐ challenged

13. When I consider who I am today (will be in the future), I feel

☐ restless   ☐ satisfied ☐ restless
(want to be   (want to be
as I was)   a new person)

My Identity

1. I believe I will be

☐ introverted ☐ outgoing

2. I believe my attitude toward strangers will be

☐ distrustful ☐ trustful

3. I believe my attitude toward my family will be

☐ loving ☐ resentful

4. I believe my view of the future will be

☐ confident ☐ expectant ☐ hopeful ☐ gloomy

5. I believe my sense of humor will be

☐ gentle ☐ rollicking ☐ sarcastic

6. I believe I will cry when I feel

☐ grieved ☐ angry ☐ ridiculed ☐ hardly ever

7. I will have the most difficulty controlling my

☐ sorrow ☐ regret ☐ fear ☐ impulsiveness ☐ anger

My Relationships with Others

1. I believe my co-workers will be

☐ searching ☐ confident

2. When I'm in a large group of people, God usually expects me to be

☐ quiet   ☐ lively   ☐ quiet   ☐ lively
  spectator   spectator   participant   participant

☐ focus of attention

3. I may have trouble getting along with

☐ other ☐ people ☐ uncommitted
   Christians   skeptics

4. I believe that when my family sees God's purpose for my life, they will

☐ approve and ☐ approve ☐ disapprove
   encourage   but not   but not
                 discourage   discourage
☐ disapprove and discourage

5. I think I will feel uncomfortable with people who are

☐ quiet people ☐ talkative people

6. I think I will feel most comfortable with people who are

☐ like me ☐ different from me

7. I believe that other people's approval will

☐ mean a ☐ concern but ☐ not guide
   great deal   make no
             difference

(Questions 8 and 9 are omitted from the scales.)

10. I believe I will have completed

☐ elementary ☐ high ☐ voc. school ☐ B.A. or
   school   school   or jr. coll.   B.S.
☐ M.A. or Ph.D.

11. I believe my annual income will be

☐ less than ☐ $10,000- ☐ $25,000- ☐ over $75,000
   $10,000 $25,000 $75,000

(Questions 12 and 13 are omitted from the scales.)

14. My house/condominium/apartment will be located in the

☐ city ☐ suburbs ☐ country

15. I believe I will be living in

☐ Northeast ☐ Midwest ☐ South ☐ West ☐ elsewhere

B. List opportunities for change.

When you have completed the scales under Part A, you will see what areas of your life you need to change the most in order to fulfill your personal goals. List the areas in which you want to begin making changes, and note some opportunities for change.

My Relationship with God

Change Needed: Opportunity for Change:

My Identity

Change Needed: Opportunity for Change:

My Relationships with Other People

Change Needed: Opportunity for Change:

C. Consider the preparation you'll need to take advantage of these opportunities.

You will need to make certain kinds of preparation to take advantage of each opportunity you listed under Part

B. Here are four basic kinds of preparation you should consider:

Knowledge. What information will I need to know in order to do this?

Insight. What will I need to understand about God, about myself, or about others in order to do this?

Sensitivity. What leadings of God or feelings of other people should I be aware of?

Conditioning. What skills will I need to learn or develop?

I call these four kinds of preparation the K-I-S-C formula. Here is how you might use the K-I-S-C formula to prepare for one of your growth opportunities:

Change Needed:
A deeper relationship with the Lord.

Opportunity for Change:
Join a Tuesday night Bible study group in my neighborhood.

Preparation I'll Need:

Knowledge: I should contact someone who is already in the group to find out where they meet, when, who leads the group, and how to join.

Insight: I should consider whether this particular Bible topic will truly help me grow. I should observe the group and perhaps visit one of their sessions, to see whether they would truly challenge me to grow.

Sensitivity: I should watch how the leader relates to the rest of the group, how the group members get along with each other, what their attitude is toward me as a newcomer, etc. And I should find out whether the Lord approves of my belonging to this group.

Conditioning: I will need to discipline myself to attend the meetings every Tuesday. I will need to set aside an hour each day for my Bible study homework. And I'll need to practice using my study Bible, so I can learn how to use the cross references and other Bible study helps in it.

As you can see, the K-I-S-C formula gives you the first steps of an action plan. Now try the K-I-S-C to begin thinking about how you can prepare for a growth opportunity in each area:

My Relationship with God

Change Needed:

Opportunity for Change:

Preparation I'll Need:

Knowledge:

Insight:

Sensitivity:

Conditioning:

D. Write your action plan.

Step C gave you the preparation phase of an action plan. When you write out a full-fledged action plan, you should be able to describe your *preparation* (how you will get ready to do it), your *implementation* (how you will do it), and your *evaluation* (how to judge the success of what you did). Take the first growth opportunity you listed under Part B and write an action plan below.

Preparation:

(Take everything you wrote under the K-I-S-C formula and list it in sequence—what you should do first, second, third and fourth to prepare for what you are planning to do.)

Implementation:

(Write a fuller description of the opportunity itself. Be specific. Exactly what do you plan to do? When will you begin? How long will you continue? Which personal goal will this activity help you reach?)

Evaluation:

(Describe the standards you will use to determine whether this activity is really helping you meet your goal. What specific changes do you expect to see in yourself or in others? How long should you wait before evaluating what you are doing? What would cause you to stop doing it? Again, be specific and realistic. Suppose I said, for example, "I'll stop if I feel I shouldn't be doing this." That would not describe what specific feelings would tell me to stop. And since all feelings are so changeable, it would be unrealistic to let my feelings tell me what I should or should not do.)

Your goals are what you intend to become; your plans are what you intend to do. Your plans grow out of your goals. To put it another way, your goals (future identity) inspire your plans (immediate course of action).

We usually look at the process from the near end, of course. Instead of thinking about whether we will be trim or obese ten years from now, we think about what we will eat for lunch today. Instead of visualizing what sort of attitude we will have toward strangers ten years from now, we elbow our way to the head of the grocery line today.

But today's impulsive actions come from the picture we have of ourselves; and when we telescope that picture a decade or so into the future and test it in light of God's Word, we begin to make intentional changes in the way we act today.

Every day we choose what we shall do; and simultaneously we choose what we shall become. The point of this book is that we can approach life the other way: We can consciously choose what we shall become, and let that guide what we choose to do.

My heart sings when I find another Christian who has made the discoveries I am making about dreams and goals. While writing this chapter I found John Powell's book, *Fully Human, Fully Alive*. Instead of dreams, Powell writes about our "visions"—how we picture ourselves in the present as well as the future. He calls the process of creative dreaming and goal-setting "vision therapy," and he says:

> If you or I are to change, to grow into persons who are more fully human and more fully alive, we shall certainly have to become more aware of our vision and patiently work at redressing its imbalances and eliminating its distortions. All real and permanent

growth must begin here. There can be no real change, no real growth in any of us until . . . our vision is changed.[4]

Every brushstroke of your daily planning should portray a bit more of your God-given purpose. Each activity can sketch in another detail of the ideal self you envision. Every day you make minor decisions that can flesh out a larger decision, a commitment you have already made to the Lord.

Keep on consulting your vision of the finished portrait to make sure each decision helps to perfect it. God has given you the vision. God leads you in defining the goals and plans that will fulfill it.

But He doesn't stop there. He also gives you the natural abilities and supernatural gifts to do all these things. Let's consider what these are.

Notes

[1] Lloyd J. Ogilvie, God's Will in Your Life (Eugene, Ore.: Harvest House Publishers, 1982), p. 73.
[2] "Lone Coal Miner Works with 2 Ponies and a Cart," The New York Times, December 11, 1983, Sec. 1, p. 44.
[3] Max Ehrmann, "Desiderata," copyright 1927, 1954, by Bertha Ehrmann.
[4] John Powell, Fully Human, Fully Alive (Allen, Tex.: Argus Communications, 1976), p. 14.

Anything will give up its secrets if you love it enough.

George Washington Carver

8

Develop Your Abilities

Queen Elizabeth I felt confident of her ability to be the Queen of England. Her keen mind unraveled the most complicated problems of state. Her discerning intuition chose leaders who ably served the Crown. Her flattering tongue reconciled the most bitter enemies of her court. She once said, "I thank God that I am endued with such qualities that if I were turned out of the Realm in my petticoat, I were able to live in any place in Christendom."

You may not feel as confident of your own abilities, but you do have them, including the ability to serve God. Your future happiness depends in large measure on how well you develop your abilities, especially your service-ability. Two well-known vocational counselors at Trinity College put it this way:

"Career satisfaction is in direct proportion to the extent people have opportunity to use their assets and abilities in achieving worthwhile goals."[1]

If you walked into a vocational counselor's office and

said, "Show me what my abilities are," the counselor would probably hand you a simple inventory form developed by the Department of Labor. Here it is, in condensed form:

Performance Skills Inventory[2]

Compared to other persons with this ability, I am probably . . .	Above Average	Average	Below Average
Reasoning—Intellectual ability. I am able to take instructions, make decisions and arrive at conclusions based on the information available.			
Verbal—Reading, speaking and listening ability. I understand what words mean and am able to communicate my ideas effectively in written or oral form.			
Numerical—Mathematical ability. I can add, subtract, multiply or divide numbers quickly and accurately.			
Spatial—Sketch interpreting			

ability. I can understand the relationship of two or more objects on a diagram or blueprint.

Form Perception —Sorting ability. I quickly see differences of size, tone or color in objects on a picture or diagram.

Clerical Perception —Proofreading ability. I quickly see errors in printed or typewritten material, and easily detect errors in arithmetic.

Motor Coordination —Manual ability. I can coordinate my hands with my eyes, performing delicate maneuvers with speed, precision and a steady hand.

Finger Dexterity —Digital ability. I can gather and assemble small objects quickly and skillfully; I can operate calculators or other small instruments swiftly and accurately.

Eye-Hand-Foot Coordination—Steering ability. I can respond quickly to what I see, using my hands and feet to operate mechanical equipment smoothly and efficiently.

Color Discrimination — Matching ability. I can recognize similarities and differences in colors, matching them or contrasting them for pleasing results.

The vocational counselor would use your answers to help you identify jobs that would call up your best abilities, whether in gardening, manufacturing, clerical work, managerial work or hundreds of other career areas. You can do the same.

In fact, you have already started. When you pictured your goals for the future, you began thinking about your abilities. When you made plans to reach your goals, you subconsciously took stock of your abilities. Though you may not have pondered it in these terms, *God calls you to a future that employs your best abilities.*

Look back at the personal goals you outlined in Chapter 6 and the plans you made for achieving these goals in Chapter 7. I believe that if they are truly Christ-honoring goals and plans, they will maximize your abilities, not muffle them.

Why? Because the Lord wastes nothing. He had a purpose for your life from the moment you were conceived, so He did not endow you with abilities to ignore or suppress or throw away. He gave you abilities that would help you fulfill His purpose.

When you visualize what sort of person God expects you to become, you find that your innate abilities are a vital part of that dream. An ability does not dictate what you should become; but like the quivering needle of a compass, it can indicate the direction you should take.

List the three areas of the Performance Skills Inventory in which you seem to have the best ability:

1.

2.

3.

Here are some occupations that may be well-suited to you if you are above average in:

Reasoning Ability. Journalism and creative writing, music, scientific research, medicine, engineering, sales, social casework and counseling, mathematics and statistics, teaching, library science, business administration, law.

Verbal Ability. Journalism and creative writing, drama, music, scientific research, medicine, engineering, sales, managerial work, social casework and counseling, mathematics and statistics, teaching, library science, business administration, law, law enforcement.

Numerical Ability. Medicine, engineering, mathematics and statistics, law, finance.

Spatial Perception. Art, scientific research, medicine, engineering, piloting, equipment operation, mathematics and statistics, athletics.

Form Perception. Art, scientific research, medicine.

Clerical Perception. Clerical work, sales, hospitality, nursing, mathematics and statistics.

Motor Coordination. Art, music, laboratory technology, barber and beauty services, crafts, athletics.

Finger Dexterity. Art, music, medicine, industrial production, crafts, athletics.

Manual Dexterity. Music, laboratory technology, agriculture, engineering, industrial production, clerical work, customer services, athletics.

Eye-Hand-Foot Coordination. Music, dancing, law enforcement, piloting, equipment operation, athletics.

Color Discrimination. Drama, barber and beauty services, interior decorating, fashion design, nursing.

A Universal Ability

God gives every person the ability to serve Him. When Scottish church leaders drew up the Westminster Shorter

Catechism to train young Christians in the basic tenets of their faith, they asked, "What is the chief end of man?" The young Christians were taught to say, "The chief end of man is to glorify God and enjoy Him forever."

Every human being's life purpose, in other words, revolves around God. We were made to reflect His design. Our deepest satisfaction is knowing that God accepts us, loves us and lives within us.

When the Father, Son and Holy Spirit consulted together to create the first man and woman, they said, "Let Us make man in Our image, according to Our likeness" (Genesis 1:26). God made everything else according to patterns He devised for the created order, but He made man according to a unique pattern. Only man has the image of God Himself in his soul, which is ready to be expressed in every person's life. Every woman and man has the innate ability to reflect God's own nature.

Even when our lives have been wrecked by sin or misfortune, we still have the image of God within. Any person can become a child of God by responding to God's revelation of Himself in Christ Jesus (John 1:12). *Any* person can! That's the glorious good news of salvation.

A Christian is a person who chooses to flesh out the image of God within him. He patterns his life after the character of God. He has "laid aside the old self with its evil practices, and . . . put on the new self who is being renewed to a true knowledge according to the image of the One who created him" (Colossians 3:9b-10).

While every person has the ability to serve God, only a Christian actually does it. Thus, the Christian develops his service-ability.

As a person exercises his ability to serve God, he becomes better able to serve. One point from Jesus' Parable of the Talents (Matthew 25:14-30) illustrates this beautifully. The manager in that parable gave his servants a supply of resources to be invested on his behalf, each according to his own ability. The servants with better managerial ability got more resources to manage. This, said Jesus, is how the Kingdom of heaven operates, too.

It seems fair enough for the man in Jesus' story to do this, but grossly unfair for God. After all, God gave us our abilities in the first place, including our service-ability; and if some people are better able to serve and glorify God, isn't it only because God gave them that extra measure of service-ability? Doesn't God determine who will be more adept at serving?

No. God enables each of us to serve Him, but He does not determine which of us will become more adept at it. We determine that ourselves. Some of us become more adept at serving God because we exercise our ability to serve Him. Even in this parable, the landowner chose men who proved they were able to serve. And to the ones who had proven their ability more than others, he gave greater responsibilities and more resources.

How to Develop Your Service-Ability

The ability to serve God is the chief ability you should develop, regardless of your aims in life. You can do it by employing each of the three aspects of service-ability—*availability, dependability* and *accountability*.

First, employ your *availability*. Army veterans are fond of saying, "Never volunteer for anything; you're bound to get hard duty." They learn that lesson when they step forward for "sit-down duty" and get a potato peeler.

But a servant in the Kingdom of God is happy to volunteer. He gladly says yes when the Master calls him to do something, even something as tedious as peeling potatoes. Jesus may call at any time because the servant is available. Are you worried about being able to do what God calls you to do? Then use your availability, and watch how He adds other abilities to your life!

Second, employ your *dependability*. Prove to the Lord that you will carry out your assignments. Show other people that they can lean on you. This is one of the most critical components of your ability to serve.

Several years back I was working as an editor at a religious publishing house. We had tight deadline schedules to meet, and I often had to call freelance writers to pick up assignments that other people had dropped. I kept the names and phone numbers of my most dependable writers in a little red book inside my shirt pocket. When a deadline stared at me from the calendar and my material had not arrived on time, I would whip out the address book and call my dependable people. I knew they would bail me out. Those were the writers I called to do the more substantial jobs, too. They had proven the quality of their work and the punctuality of their service. It made good business sense to call on dependable people.

It makes good sense in the Kingdom of God, too. As we saw in Jesus' parable, the people who prove their service will be asked for more service. When God knows He can count on you, He gives you more responsibility.

Finally, employ your *accountability*. Be ready to answer to God for the way you are living. Live and serve in such a way that you would never be ashamed to give Him a personal report of your day's activities. You are continually accounting to someone for the way you live. You are trying to please someone. The crucial question is, Are you trying to please the Lord?

Here, then, are three ways to develop your ability to serve God: by exercising your availability, your dependability, and your accountability whenever He calls you to serve. An athlete tones up his muscles by going to a health spa or gym every week to lift weights or flex the springs. Likewise, you can tone up your most basic ability as a servant to the King by exercising it. You become better able to do God's will by doing His will. You become more adept at finding God's will by following His will.

When you gave your life to the Lord He ushered you into the training room of service, and you will become better able to serve Him by serving Him.

Notes

[1] Kirk E. Farnsworth and Wendell H. Lawhead, *Life Planning* (Downers Grove, Ill.: InterVarsity Press, 1981), p. 50.

[2] Based on the *Dictionary of Occupational Titles,* Vol. II, Third Ed. (Washington, D.C.: U.S. Government Printing Office, 1965), p. 653.

*If some service I am performing is help-
ing other Christians in a significant way or
bringing others to Christ, then it is quite
likely I am making use of a spiritual gift.*
M. Blaine Smith[1]

9

Discover Your Gifts

My wife has a creative sense of playfulness. That is one
thing that attracted me to Judy: I can always count on her
to devise an enjoyable way to do things.

A few months ago Judy hosted a wedding shower and
decided to give her present to the prospective bride in an
unusual way: Instead of wrapping the present and putting
it on the table with the other gifts, she hid it and gave the
bride clues to where it was. The first clue directed her
friend to the place she could find the second clue, and so
on. After about half-a-dozen clues, she found her gift—a
Mexican wall hanging, mounted on the wall behind the
door. She had walked right by it on her way in without
knowing it was there!

Often we have gifts we don't realize, too—spiritual gifts
that are right under our noses. Jesus has given them to us

as Christians, yet we may not know we have them until
someone points them out. As Paul wrote,

> But to each one of us grace was given according to
> the measure of Christ's gift. . . . And He gave some as
> apostles, and some as prophets, and some as evan-
> gelists, and some as pastors and teachers, for the
> equipping of the saints for the work of service, to the
> building up of the body of Christ; until we all attain to
> the unity of the faith, and of the knowledge of the Son
> of God, to a mature man, to the measure of the
> stature which belongs to the fulness of Christ.
>   (Ephesians 4:7, 11-13)

There are at least four things to keep in mind in any
discussion of spiritual gifts.

First, *these gifts come from Christ.* He is the One who
"ascended on high" (verse 8). Thus, any special spiritual
abilities you have were given to you by Him.

Second, *Christ granted these gifts to celebrate His victory over sin,* as Paul points out in the same chapter. Try to
picture this in your mind. It is as if Jesus Christ were a
conquering general in battle. When He ascended into
heaven, He led behind Him the captives of death and hell
and sin, which He conquered when He rose from the
dead. They no longer have power over Him or His followers. And as part of His victory celebration, Jesus gave
gifts to us.

In New Testament times, as a conquering general rode
through the streets in his victory parade, he tossed trophies of battle to his supporters who stood along the
way—silver, gold, precious fabrics and other objects he
had captured. People clamored for these like children
scrambling for candy. It was the custom of the day.

And this is exactly what Jesus did when He ascended into heaven: He tossed out the trophies of battle to you and me. What were those trophies? Spiritual gifts.

The third thing to remember about spiritual gifts is that *a Christian receives special ability to do whatever God calls him to do.* Notice again that Ephesians 4:12 says our spiritual gifts are "for the equipping of the saints for the work of service." You don't need to worry about being able to answer God's calling, because He will give you the proper equipment to do the task.

My brother used to be a company clerk for the Quartermaster Corps at Fort Benning, Georgia. As raw recruits came into the induction station, it was Dan's job to muster out their gear. Every new soldier was equipped for service with a uniform, pack, shovel, pair of shoes and so on.

Imagine, if you will, that Jesus Christ is your spiritual Quartermaster. When you report for duty in His Kingdom, He equips you for duty. That is what the Bible says here.

The fourth point Paul makes is that *Jesus grants spiritual gifts for "building up the Body of Christ."* He gives you special abilities not for your benefit, but to benefit other Christians. They are service abilities, not self-service abilities.

The same could be said of *any* gift. When you plunge into the crowd at a shopping mall to find a Christmas gift for someone, your first thought is, "What would she really like?" But your second thought is, "What would benefit the people around her?" If you think I am exaggerating, consider some gifts that might have been under your Christmas tree last year. That bottle of perfume for your aunt, for example, had a delightful fragrance. She enjoys wearing it because she likes the smell. But don't the people around her enjoy it, too?

I venture to say that most gifts are an asset to the people

who receive them, but to other people as well. So it is with spiritual gifts.

I underscore this point because I think some Christians spend too much time attending seminars and reading books that help them develop their spiritual gifts without employing them for the good of the Body. As a result, other Christians don't care about discovering their gifts because it often seems a self-centered hobby.

Christ gives spiritual gifts to equip the saints and build up the Body. He makes sure that no Christian has all the service gifts. He distributes them throughout the fellowship, so we have to depend on each other. It is an ingenious plan!

Gifts vs. Talents

Some people have an innate ability to talk in a constructive way. They have the talent known as loquacity. They can begin a conversation and keep it going; they know interesting things to talk about; they can draw out the ideas of the other person.

Some people have the innate ability of listening, too, which is just as important as the gift of gab. (If God had not given as many people the ability to listen as He did the ability to talk, it would be a frustrating world, wouldn't it?)

But inborn abilities are not what Paul is talking about in his letter to the Ephesians. The text describes gifts Christ gave us when He triumphed over sin; and that triumph applies to us only after we are converted. Christ's victory means nothing for you until you give your heart to Him. At that moment, you receive the gifts He made available. You receive His special equipment "for the work of service" (Ephesians 4:12).

But it is usually harder to discern spiritual gifts than it is natural abilities such as loquacity. We tend to praise a Christian's talents since they are evident, and our praise encourages him to exercise his talents even more. But we stumble over one another's spiritual gifts quite by accident.

We do not know that the quiet, smartly dressed young woman who sits in the back pew has a gift for administration until we ask her to organize a telephone campaign. We don't know that the balding, fiftyish bachelor has a gift for teaching until we ask him to substitute for the junior high Sunday school teacher one morning. Talents are obvious; spiritual gifts are hidden. And I believe many churches have burned out more than a few willing workers because they have not tried to discover and employ more of these workers' spiritual gifts.

The Goal of God's Church

Ephesians 4:13 says we should use our spiritual gifts in serving one another so that we may attain "the measure of the stature which belongs to the fulness of Christ." This is the goal of the Church. Individually and as a body, we are called to become like Christ Himself.

Many years ago C. W. Naylor wrote a song entitled "More Like Christ." Here is the first stanza:

> More like Christ my heart is praying,
> More like Christ from day to day,
> All His graces rich displaying
> While I tread this pilgrim way.

Every Christian should aim to become more like Christ, who is the measure of spiritual maturity. It is important for each of us to discover and develop our God-given gifts that help all of us become more like Christ.

The apostle Paul told his young friend Timothy, "Stir up the gift of God which is in you" (II Timothy 1:6, NKJV). I like the New International Version rendering of that: "Fan into flame the gift of God, which is in you." You have been specially gifted to help other Christians grow. And when you have identified that gift, do everything you can to enhance it. Fan the spark of your spiritual gift into a blazing flame for Christ.

Do you suppose some Christians have no gift? Then read Ephesians 4:7: "To each one of us grace was given according to the measure of Christ's gift." Every Christian, in other words, has a spiritual gift. Christ Himself chose the gift that would be best for you, the one you could use to glorify Him most fully.

The Lord has no unequipped servants. To put it another way, He has no "generic" Christians.

Many supermarkets now carry generic products: canned foods, boxed cereals, facial tissues, paper towels and other items with no brand names. Each has a plain wrapper with the contents labeled in simple block letters. They have no color, no flair, no special ingredients. Just the basic, generic "stuff."

But God makes no generic Christians. Each Christian is unique. Jesus Christ has given you service gifts that set you apart from every other Christian. Perhaps you have failed to notice your gifts; perhaps they have never been employed. But the Word of God guarantees that you have one!

Let's Take Inventory

Arlo F. Newell has given us an instructive study of spiritual gifts in his book *Receive the Holy Spirit.*[2] He notes three general classes of New Testament spiritual gifts:

Speaking gifts (e.g., prophesying and teaching)
Serving gifts (e.g., administration and helping)
Signifying gifts (e.g., tongues and miracles)[3]

These classifications are easy to remember, and they prompt us to think about some spiritual gifts that are not listed in the Bible itself. A Christian with a gift for counseling can listen intently while someone describes a personal problem and then offer good advice; his *speaking* gift helps that person grow. Another Christian with a gift for playing musical instruments can do much to enhance a worship service; his *serving* gift helps us grow.

The Bible does not list counseling or playing instruments among the spiritual gifts, but they certainly have that function. They build up other Christians toward maturity in Christ.

Here are a few pen-and-paper exercises to help you take inventory of your spiritual gifts, using Dr. Newell's categories:

Formal Church Life

Informal Church Life

Under the heading *Formal Church Life*, give a brief description of every official church duty you have performed. (Include teaching a class, making announcements in a worship service, counseling someone in a prayer room, serving refreshments, washing dishes after potluck dinners—everything!) Put an asterisk (*) beside each one that you seemed to have a special knack for doing.

Under the section *Informal Church Life,* describe everything you have done to serve your Christian brothers and sisters outside the church's normal weekly routine—those spur-of-the-moment duties you have performed for other Christians on the impulse of love. Examples might be staying at the bedside of a sick friend, preparing a meal for a bereaved family, writing cards of encouragement, counseling someone over the phone, and so on. Again, put an asterisk beside each function that you seemed to do especially well.

Now list every duty you marked with an asterisk under one of the three Spiritual Gift headings.

Speaking Gifts   Serving Gifts   Signifying Gifts

Here is an example of how your list might look:

Speaking Gifts	Serving Gifts	Signifying Gifts
*Teaching S.S. class	*Washing dishes	*Praying for healing
*Visiting absentees	*Mending curtains	
	*Staying w/ invalid	
	*Sending cards	

Are more of your items clustered under one heading?

That suggests your spiritual gifts lie in that area. The sample above belongs to a person with strong serving gifts; if he tries to engage in other kinds of personal service, he might uncover even more gifts.

The best way to discover your spiritual gifts is to exercise them by trying them out in your local congregation. I hope you worship with a group of Christians who will risk letting you try something you have never tried before. You might fail. On the other hand, you might prove to have an extraordinary gift you didn't even know about!

Early in this book, I said that developing your goals and plans might be likened to developing a photograph. You might also say that spiritual gifts are the darkroom equipment of your life; they bring out the character traits God gave you.

Someone observed that the well-known nature photographer Ansel Adams was able to render a particular scene in a variety of ways by using the same negative but different chemicals, filters and papers in the darkroom. Adams himself said, "The negative is the score. The print is the performance."

So it is with spiritual gifts: Your life goal is your score, but you can render it any number of ways depending on how you employ your spiritual gifts.

Duty and Delight

Every gift brings responsibilities. The Christian who discovers his gifts feels uncomfortable till he begins using them as the Lord intended. He is like the Old Testament prophet who said that prophecy was "like a burning fire shut up in my bones" (Jeremiah 20:9).

Every gift has its privileges, too. News reporters in Washington, D.C., have long complained about the special privileges that come with high office: private limousine service, heated pools, plush lounges, trips abroad. But some executive privileges are essential. Who would quarrel with the President's need for a bodyguard? Or the senators' need for couriers?

Consider the executive privileges that Christians have. A Christian with the gift of praying for the sick has the privilege of seeing them healed. A Christian with the gift of counseling has the thrill of seeing people find God's will for their lives. A Christian with the gift of administration has the satisfaction of resolving difficult problems within the church.

When you feel weighed down by your duties in the Body of Christ, remember your gifts! And relish their privileges—executive privileges!

Notes

[1] M. Blaine Smith, *Knowing God's Will* (Downers Grove, Ill.: InterVarsity Press, 1979), p. 98.

[2] Arlo F. Newell, *Receive the Holy Spirit* (Anderson, Ind.: Warner Press, 1978), p. 90.

[3] The signifying gifts are commonly called "charismatic" gifts. I dislike that phrase because it singles out a few spiritual gifts as if they were of a different quality than the rest. The word *charismatic* means "pertaining to gifts." All spiritual gifts, therefore, might be called charismatic because all are given by God.

Some of us may be fearing the wrong thing. What we fear most is the pain that is necessary for our own growth.

William E. Hulme[1]

10

When You Need to Change Your Plans

A widow I knew from church began making some bold changes in her life plans about three years ago. Her children had married or gone away to college. She had no further obligations in Fort Wayne. So she decided to sell her house and begin helping other people wherever she might be needed.

She spent several months caring for an invalid friend in Fort Wayne. She helped her oldest son start a new congregation in Virginia. She served as a cook at a Christian retreat center in Tennessee. Then she worked at a Christian nursery school in Louisville.

When she returned to church for our Christmas Eve service, I said, "Mona Jean, you're just like the wise men following the star. They didn't know their destination. They just knew they were going in the right direction."

Perhaps that describes your life, too. You often need to change your life plans; and occasionally the changes are so abrupt that you may feel a little puzzled about how your life will turn out. But you are sure you are going in the right direction.

The apostle Paul had this experience. He knew God wanted him to be a bold spokesman for Jesus Christ and a shepherd of the new congregations springing up throughout the Roman world. God changed his plans many times. Indeed, Paul's life ended much sooner than he expected and in a way he did not expect. Yet he knew these changes were part of God's purpose for his life. He knew his life was going in the right direction, even when the executioner's axe fell.

A Change of Itinerary

The first chapter of II Corinthians describes a painful change in Paul's plans. Paul was making his third missionary journey, visiting the churches scattered around the Mediterranean. He planned to go to Corinth, a troubled church, to see if they had made any progress toward resolving the problems he observed in his first visit with them. Then he planned to proceed to Macedonia, make a circuit of the churches in that region, and finally return to Corinth to receive an offering for the famine-stricken churches in Judea.

But while Paul was visiting the churches in Asia Minor, he was stricken with a grave health problem. He writes of an "affliction which came to us in Asia" (II Corinthians 1:8), saying that "we were burdened excessively, beyond our strength, so that we despaired even of life."

Perhaps Paul had a physical or emotional collapse, exhausted by the nerve-wracking schedule. Perhaps he had a flare-up of his "thorn in the flesh," an unidentified malady he mentions later in II Corinthians 12:7-10. Perhaps he had a heart attack or stroke. Whatever his life-threatening affliction, Paul says only that it required a long period of recovery.

This health trouble gave Paul time to think. He decided not to visit Corinth after all, and sent his young associate Titus instead. He told his Corinthian friends that he had decided, on second thought, not to check up on them; that they might grow more mature if he spared them a "bawling-out."

God assured Paul that this was the best thing to do. Circumstances had forced a change in his plan. Reflection showed him what the change should be. And God confirmed that the change would glorify Him. So Paul explains in his letter to the Corinthians two different ways he sensed the Lord's confirmation of his new plan.

First, God gave him *confidence*.

Our proud confidence is this, the testimony of our conscience, that in holiness and godly sincerity, not in fleshly wisdom but in the grace of God, we have conducted ourselves in the world, and especially toward you.

(II Corinthians 1:12)

Paul had a clear conscience about changing his plans; he knew he had made his decision with sincere, God-fearing intent.

George Newton, Jr., my pastor in Nashville, often closed a worship service by asking, "Are all hearts clear?" He knew God was convicting the hearts of some people who had heard the gospel preached that day, yet had refused to make a clear decision. So Pastor Newton offered that final challenge.

God will give you a clear conscience when you are doing His will. He will assure you that, even though you have had to change your course of action, you are doing the right thing.

The second way God confirmed Paul's decision was by showing him *positive results*. Paul congratulated the Corinthians "for in your faith you are standing firm" (verse 24). He had yearned to see the Corinthians grow up, emotionally and spiritually. By canceling his plans to visit them, he had forced them to take responsibility for their actions. Granted, they were still immature in many respects, but they were staying true to Jesus Christ. This result alone told Paul he had made the right decision.

Notice that Paul does not say God used a dream, vision or prophetic revelation to tell him what to do, although in other epistles he talks freely about receiving guidance through those channels. Instead, Paul says he made the decision "in holiness and godly sincerity." While following the intentions of a sincere, godly heart, in other words, Paul considered the facts, reviewed what he hoped to accomplish for the Lord, and concluded that the best way to achieve his purpose was to cancel his trip to Corinth.

Notice, too, that Paul made his decision *before* he had God's guarantee that it was the best plan. Both confirmations—his clear conscience and the good results—came after Paul's decision to bypass Corinth.

We usually have to make our decisions, too, with simply the facts in hand and a heart burning to do what is right. God will confirm our decision afterward, but at the moment of decision we have to trust our own best judgment. M. Blaine Smith writes:

In the overwhelming majority of decisions noted in the New Testament God's will was discerned through a reasoned decision. Human reason was the channel through which God's will was normally known; discerning his will boiled down to a matter of making a sound, logical choice.[2]

We might debate whether it was actually God who changed Paul's plans. "After all," you might say, "Paul had to revise his plans because of the circumstances, and circumstances don't always reveal the will of God."

So they don't. Circumstances alone cannot show us God's plans. But circumstances force us to reconsider our plans. If Paul had not fallen ill, he might have camped in Corinth for months, trying to untangle the problems of that church. And Paul's illness forced him to reconsider that plan; it challenged him to ask himself, "Might there be a better way to help the Corinthians?"

We can debate whether God caused Paul his "great adversity." But one thing is clear: God prevailed upon Paul in the adversity to find a better plan of action. He guided Paul's heart. Paul chose a better plan because adversity prompted further thinking, and a holy heart guided his thinking.

Modern Examples of Revised Plans

It is painful to change your plans, especially if you have invested much fervor in the original plan or talked it up with your friends. It is hard to change career plans, marital plans or any plan that you have expected earnestly to fulfill. But God may call His servants to change their plans at some point, no matter how ingenious and perfect they had seemed.

Circumstances may force such a change, as in the case of Joyce Landorf we looked at earlier. She was forced to suspend a successful ministry of singing and lecturing because of a painful jaw ailment, only to discover a new and broader ministry of writing.

In other cases we may opt for a change, even though circumstances don't demand it. I had lunch recently with a good friend who was making an abrupt change in his career. He had been a pastor, then an editor at a Christian publishing house. Then he attended a retreat where he assessed his personal goals and realized that he secretly yearned to be a pastor again.

An attractive college church asked him to consider becoming their pastor. He visited the church, saw how much he enjoyed using his pastoral gifts, and decided in a few days to accept their call.

"I'm surprised it happened so fast," he told me over tossed salad. "I knew I might go back to pastoral work someday, but I had told myself I would stick with the editorial job for at least two more years."

"Why?" I asked.

"I felt I owed that much to my publishing firm."

"So what convinced you to change your plans?"

"The Lord did," he smiled. "I would have betrayed the gifts He gave me if I stayed in publishing out of a sheer sense of duty. I'll have some regrets about leaving. There may be days I'll wonder if I made the right decision. But I've decided to make the best of what the Lord has given me."

You might say my friend made an *elective* change of plans, since nothing forced him to do it. His superiors at the publishing house were pleased with his work. His wife and family were supportive. He could have stayed there indefinitely. But he yielded to his God-given dream of returning to the pastorate.

You may be facing a change of plans right now. Whether it is an elective change or one forced by your circumstances, remember this: You can still achieve your goals and become the person God expects you to be, even though the details of your future may not be what you had pictured.

Two Extremes to Avoid

Some people are given to change. They like to rearrange their careers, marriages or friendships almost as often as they rearrange the furniture in their living rooms. The Bible says to avoid such people; they make life a shambles for themselves and for you (Proverbs 24:21).

On the other end of the spectrum are people who refuse to change their life plans. They are miserable as they are, but afraid that a different way of life would be even more miserable. They say, "At least I know how to deal with the mess I'm in." So they grit their teeth and hang on.

A healthy, mature Christian lives between those two extremes. He does not change his lifestyle flippantly every few months, but he does not dig in his heels and refuse to change, either. A healthy Christian accepts change as a natural part of life. He is flexible enough to adapt to adversity and ambitious enough to take opportunity. Either way he pursues his personal goals to honor the Lord.

God's Will, God's Word and Your Plans

When you need to change your life plans, you come to

grips with a question that has occupied theologians for centuries: *How can I know God's will for my life?*

Instead of trying to provide a pat answer, I invite you once again to use your imagination. How do you visualize God revealing His will to you? Do you see Him writing you a letter, setting down explicit directions in A-B-C fashion?

"God has already given me a set of directions like that," you might say. "It's called the Bible."

But that oversimplifies things a bit. The Bible does indeed give many explicit commands and promises. But God has directed His Word to all people who have ever lived, so that, for example, Mary Johnson cannot expect to open the Bible and find a list of personal assignments for May 25th of this year.

Of course, some Christians like to think they can use the Bible in that way. They suppose the Bible has mystical power to direct their lives. If they want guidance for a specific decision, they browse through the Bible, or open it at random, until they find a text that seems to give them the answer.

That method treats the Bible as if it were a kind of divine ouija board. It is not.

The Bible does indeed contain God's general commands for all mankind and His specific commands for a Christian. It says, for example, that marriage is an honorable option for any person (Hebrews 13:4). It warns that a Christian should not marry an unsaved person (II Corinthians 6:14). But the Bible does not say whether *you* should marry. And if it comes down to a choice of marrying Gail or Marsha, both of whom are fine Christian girls, the Bible does not specify which girl to choose. In these matters, you must seek God's will directly from Him.

If God's will does not come to you as a neat set of written directions, then, how does it come? Paul E. Little wrote,

The will of God is . . . like a scroll that unrolls every day. In other words, God has a will for you and me today and tomorrow and the next day and the day after that. . . . It may well be that a decision we make this week or next week will commit us for three months, or two years, or five or ten years, or for a lifetime. But the fact still remains that the will of God is something to be discerned and to be lived out each day of our lives. It is not something to be grasped as a package once for all.[3]

I like this scroll analogy. When a Jewish rabbi searches for a verse on one of the huge synagogue scrolls, he spools the parchment patiently from one roll to the other until he finds the place. He can see only a small portion of the text at one time, although he knows the rest is there, wound on the rolls.

That is how you can perceive God's plan for your life, too. You see only the immediate plan—what He leads you to do today—even though you know there is more of His will not yet revealed.

And if you imagine God's will as a scroll, unrolling a bit more every day, you can expect some surprises now and then. Your life will be full of unexpected changes. Your goals will seem always beyond your grasp, challenging you to grow. But you continue on because you have decided that your journey is worth the pain of change, and the frustration of continual challenge.

I believe it was Teilhard de Chardin who said, "Since I started following Jesus, He has led me places I never expected to go." Every Christian could say that. Life is full of surprises when you are traveling with Jesus!

Notes

[1] William E. Hulme, *Dealing with Double-Mindedness* (New York: Harper & Row, 1982), p. 24.

[2] M. Blaine Smith, *Knowing God's Will* (Downers Grove, Ill.: InterVarsity Press, 1979), p. 61.

[3] Paul E. Little, *Affirming the Will of God* (Downers Grove, Ill.: InterVarsity Press, 1971), pp. 7-8.

Start to live the kind of life God can bless, where you are. Don't wait until next month or next year for the opportunity that may make you great.

Robert A. Cook[1]

11

Face Forward—

It's Not Too Soon to Start!

Recent changes in our world have forced many Christians to reexamine their goals and plans.

Factories have shut down, throwing thousands of people out of work; and in many cases, those jobs have simply disappeared. In my former hometown of Fort Wayne, International Harvester began laying off a work force of more than 10,000 people in the summer of 1980. Every kind of worker was affected—brawny men who worked on the assembly line and brilliant engineers who labored in the front office. But they all said, "What's to worry? Business will pick up in a few months. They'll call us back to work."

The heavy truck business did not pick up, however, and

in September 1983 officials announced the Fort Wayne plant would be closed and sold. As I write these words, thousands of laid-off Fort Wayne workers are sitting at home, stunned by the news. Their industry has changed and now they, too, must change.

Family patterns have also undergone tremendous change. No longer can we take for granted the traditional image of the family we saw in Norman Rockwell's cover drawings for the *Saturday Evening Post*—a father, mother, two grandparents and rosy-cheeked children sitting down to a festive table laden with food. That seldom happens anymore. There may be only one parent at the head of the table; the menu is probably more meager; and the grandparents may live far across the country. Our families have changed, and now we must change.

Medical science has changed our way of life, too. New technology and drugs allow us to fight off diseases and recover from accidents that would have claimed our lives twenty years ago. We can probably look forward to a retirement period of thirty years or more. We can expect to spend part of our lives in a nursing home or other extended-care facility. Mentally or physically handicapped relatives may be able to live at home now, since we have the equipment and medication to care for them there. All these medical advances are bringing about dramatic changes in our lifestyle. Our physical lives have changed, and now we must change.

We are experiencing more radical changes than any generation has ever known. We have more options than any generation has known. Necessity and opportunity are like the two wedges of a vise, squeezing our lives out of their old shape. But what will be the new shape of our lives? How can we set goals that will be reasonable, achievable and pleasing to the Lord? These are the questions we have been attempting to answer.

No Future in the Past

One thing is certain: We cannot construct our future by trying to patch up the past. If we try, we will find ourselves in the predicament of the American novelist Thomas Wolfe, who grew up in the quaint mountain town of Asheville, North Carolina. After making a successful career in the North, he decided to return to Asheville. But the town had changed. No longer a sleepy little village in the foothills of the Appalachians, it had become a bustling trade center and neon-lighted tourist attraction. The novelist concluded sadly that the town where he now wanted to live existed only in his memory; the real Asheville was very different from the one he remembered.

Thomas Wolfe was different, too. Strangers hailed him on the street and clamored for his autograph. Ambitious young writers pursued him with their manuscripts. He felt as though he were on public exhibit. No longer could he enjoy the quiet solitude he had known as a youth sitting on a park bench in Asheville. He became suspicious, defensive and cynical. So Wolfe returned to New York and wrote the book *You Can't Go Home Again,* a kind of personal confession. He learned he could not return to the past, no matter how desperately he tried.

None of us can. We may want to recapture the past because it is familiar and predictable and safe. But regardless of how hard we try, we cannot make our future in the past. The surroundings are different; we are different. We may try to pick up life where we left off twenty years before, but it's no use. We cannot resurrect the past.

The Pharisees once asked why Jesus' disciples did not act like those of John the Baptist. Jesus replied,

"No one sews a patch of unshrunk cloth on an old garment; otherwise the patch pulls away from it, the new from the old, and a worse tear results. And no one puts new wine into old wineskins; otherwise the wine will burst the skins, and the wine is lost, and the skins as well; but one puts new wine into fresh wineskins."

(Mark 2:21-22)

Jesus called His men to a completely new way of life—a freer, more joyful one. The traditionalists could not understand this. They thought that if certain disciplines had been good enough for John's disciples, they should be good enough for anyone. But Jesus freed His followers from conformity. He encouraged them to adopt a lifestyle that allowed them to serve Him most faithfully, even if other holy men did not live that way!

Please understand. I am not telling you to adopt some exotic lifestyle to prove you are a Christian. I am not saying you should offend traditionalists to demonstrate that you are different from them. That is not what Jesus meant. His point was this: Honoring the past and honoring other people are not a Christian's top priority. Honoring the Lord is.

I believe we honor the Lord by answering His "upward call" into the future. The apostle Paul lived this way. Near the end of his life, he wrote to his Christian friends at Philippi, encouraging them to stay true to the Lord. "I count all things to be loss in view of the surpassing value of knowing Christ Jesus my Lord," he wrote in Philippians 3:8. Even though he had experienced many wonderful things in God's service, he did not intend to spend the rest of his life fondling memories.

Thus, he wrote:

> . . . Forgetting what lies behind and reaching forward to what lies ahead, I press on toward the goal for the prize of the upward call of God in Christ Jesus.
> (Philippians 3:13-14)

God was calling him upward, onward and forward. Paul did not intend to rest on his laurels. No, he was going forward with Christ!

We can be sure that Paul lived vibrantly and radiantly in that spirit until the day of his death. So long as he followed the upward call of Christ, he had challenging new goals and plans for each day.

I believe God wants every Christian to live that way. He expects us to reflect His character more perfectly every day of our lives. I believe He intends for us to be goal-oriented, future-tending people who strive to become more like Him.

"That Sounds Good, But. . . ."

You may feel intimidated by the whole idea of goal-setting, especially if it challenges you to make radical changes in the way you live. I understand how you feel. I have often felt the same way. But when I read how other people made dramatic life changes for the Lord, I take courage to dream godly dreams and set godly goals.

The saints of Bible times were also uneasy about setting godly goals. In fact, when God gave them stirring dreams for the future they made excuses not to dream. Excuses like:

"I'm too old." The priest Zacharias prayed for a son so long that he assumed his prayer could not be answered. Then one day an angel appeared to him at the altar and predicted his wife would bear a son. "How shall I know this for certain?" Zacharias asked in wonder. "For I am an old man, and my wife is advanced in years" (Luke 1:18). Yet the old priest's wife bore a son, John the Baptist. Zacharias became a father at an age long after most men would despair of having children.

"I don't have what it takes." When God called Moses to confront the pharaoh of Egypt, he replied, "I am slow of speech and slow of tongue" (Exodus 4:10). He did not feel he could speak persuasively enough to the mighty builder of the pyramids. But God said, "Who has made man's mouth? . . . Is it not I, the Lord? Now then go, and I, even I, will be with your mouth, and teach you what you are to say" (verses 11-12). Moses learned he did not have to be an eloquent speaker, just a faithful one. And God gave him what to say.

"I'm too committed to this way of life." Simon Peter knew Jesus was calling him to be a disciple; he had been able to evade Jesus' call. But when he saw Jesus' miracles, he had to say something. "Depart from me," he cried, "for I am a sinful man, O Lord!" (Luke 5:8). He felt he could keep on tending his nets more easily than embark on a totally new way of life. But the Lord said, "Do not fear, from now on you will be catching men" (verse 10).

Do these excuses sound familiar? They do to me, because I have used them myself!

But Jesus Christ calls us forward. He calls us to let go of what is behind; that is forgiven. He calls us to reach out toward the dream; that is foreseen. He calls us to shape our character after His; that is foremost in His will for our lives.

A goal-oriented life may be painful. It may be checkered with failure and disappointment. But Christ promises great reward when we walk with Him, face forward to eternity.

> "For this reason I say to you, do not be anxious for your life, as to what you shall eat; nor for your body, as to what you shall put on. For life is more than food, and the body than clothing.
> "And do not seek what you shall eat, and what you shall drink, and do not keep worrying. For all these things the nations of the world eagerly seek; but your Father knows that you need these things. But seek for His kingdom, and these things shall be added to you. Do not be afraid, little flock, for your Father has chosen gladly to give you the kingdom."
> (Luke 12:22-23, 29-32)

At the beginning of this book, you may have viewed goal-setting in terms of material goals—what type of job you would like to have, what kind of home you would like to own, what style of clothes you would like to wear, and so on. But these things are not the heart of your future; they are merely the background details. The heart of the matter is this: *What sort of person will you become?*

To live as a servant of the King, reflecting the character of the King—that is the essence of Christian living. And the Father has chosen gladly to give you that kind of living. You can begin fulfilling that goal today.

Notes

[1] Robert A. Cook, *Now That I Believe* (Chicago: Moody Press, 1949), p. 107.

Epilogue

This book changed my life. It led me to reexamine my own life goals and make crucial changes in my life plans.

When I began writing it, I was in the fourth year of my pastorate in Fort Wayne. The Lord was blessing my ministry. By every measure, my congregation was growing in spiritual maturity and outreach. I was happy in my work. My people seemed happy with me.

But I had not given serious thought to my life goals. I was not sure what sort of person God expected me to become, so my short-range plans were haphazard and I was not sure how to measure my personal growth.

I had preached a series of sermons on "How to Set Goals for Your Life" because several of my parishoners had lost their jobs during the most recent recession, and they needed to get their bearings for the future. I had dug into Scripture to give them some practical words about divine guidance and goal-setting.

The sermons helped. So I decided to write a book on the subject. I dug deeper into the Word. And I soon realized that God was challenging me to take a close look at my own goals.

I concluded that although pastoral ministry was a good

avenue of service for me, I was being called back into Christian publishing.

That conviction grew during the eight months I wrote and rewrote this book. Then the phone rang. It was the associate publisher at The Zondervan Corporation, who wondered if I might consider Christian publishing work again. We talked. I told him I was open to the idea. Then I asked how he had gotten my name. He had come by way of a pastor in Seattle, another former editor for whom I had written some Sunday school curriculum five years earlier!

After several interviews, undergirded by prayer and thought, I chose to accept a new editorial position at Zondervan. Even now I am in the process of moving. And tonight, before sitting at the desk to write these words, I agreed to sell my house to a Christian couple from Cleveland—just four days after staking the *For Sale* sign out front!

Some people would say these are interesting coincidences. Perhaps. But I believe God used the process of goal-setting to prepare me for that phone call . . . that interview . . . that visit tonight . . . and many other surprising turns of His will.

He can do the same with you.